After the Whirlwind

Thomas J. Watkins

&

Parson's Porch Books

www.parsonsporchbooks.com

After the Whirlwind
ISBN: Softcover 978-1-949888-95-9
Copyright © 2019 by Thomas J. Watkins

After the Whirlwind

Contents

Preaching Themes

Introduction

It was in a small church in Wendell, North Carolina where I learned the discipline of weekly preaching. The church, at the time, was essentially a one-room schoolhouse. The pulpit was a lectern. The pews were chairs, with the first row three feet from my toes. The congregation was so close that I could see every shift, scratch and passed note. Families with young children would sit on the first row so their kids could have space to play at their feet... and mine. One Sunday, a seven-year-old boy took his spot on that front row with his family and managed well enough through the first part of the service. I moved to the lectern to start the sermon. As I began arranging my notes, the boy groaned, "Oh no. This is the part I *hate!*" This book is dedicated to that child. Children will say what no one says but what everyone is thinking... including the preacher!

Preaching is hard work. It isn't designing rockets, and I imagine almost everyone has some capacity to stand up and talk for twenty minutes. Still, to develop a thoughtful oration drawn out of ancient texts that speaks creatively to a contemporary, diverse audience is an obvious challenge. It is even more of a challenge in a world in which everyone else has already given up that model of presentation. Few others talk without props for twenty minutes to people who sit silently in stiff pews. My friend Art Ross refers to it as the "relentless return of Sunday."

I've read theories of preaching and heard lectures about preaching principals. I do not have any of those things - theories or principals. I thank God every Sunday for the Holy Spirit because without it I honestly don't know how anyone could engage the same preacher week after week. I also thank God every Sunday for the Holy Scriptures because I do know there is an expanse to God's Word that still speaks to the human experience if we are willing to dig deeper and deeper. Sometimes the preacher has to get out of the lectionary. Sometimes she has to stay with it one more time, for yet another reading on John the Baptist, though she has preached on him a zillion times already. Sometimes the preacher is like the comedian who looks for the one thing that is "off." That is what I often do in the preaching moment, find the piece in the passage that stands out and explore it.

The sermons gathered for this volume represent about a year's worth of preaching, all at First Presbyterian Church of Wilson, North Carolina. The sermons are categorized into three areas: Preaching Books, Preaching Seasons and Preaching Themes.

Preachers can be quite narcissistic, assuming the world just can't wait to hear what we have to say. That's why Parson's Porch Books will never run out of the preachers willing to submit their finest work! Nonetheless, I am grateful to David Russell Tullock for reaching out to me and encouraging me to complete this task. I am grateful to the congregation of First Presbyterian for our ministry together and for their willingness to hear this preacher almost every week. I am grateful to the members of Covenant Presbyterian in Wendell, North Carolina and White Memorial Presbyterian in Raleigh who trained me as a preacher. And I am grateful for many other congregations but especially Shades Valley Presbyterian of Birmingham for nurturing me as a disciple of Christ.

I am always and especially grateful to my wife, Julie, and our children, Mary Thomas and Jack. Their love and support are precious, as is their ability to correct my ego if it rises above the steps of pulpit. One Sunday after church, Jack and I went to the store to pick up items to bring home for lunch. A church lady, fresh out of worship, grabbed me in the parking lot. "Tom, that was the best sermon I have ever heard!" As I then attempted to shove my enormous head back into my car, my son, already inside, deadpanned, "I've heard better." "You don't even listen to them," I barked. "Give me something to listen to," he said. Such is the task of the relentless return of Sunday.

Preaching Books

In the Land of Uz

Job 1:1, 2:1-10

There was once a man in the land of Uz whose name was Job. That man was blameless and upright, one who feared God and turned away from evil.

One day the heavenly beings came to present themselves before the LORD, and Satan also came among them to present himself before he LORD. ² The LORD said to Satan, "Where have you come from?" Satan answered the LORD, "From going to and fro on the earth, and from walking up and down on it." ³ The LORD said to Satan," Have you considered my servant Job? There is no one like him on the earth, a blameless and upright man who fears God and turns away from evil. He still persists in his integrity, although you incited me against him, to destroy him for no reason." ⁴ Then Satan answered the LORD, "Skin for skin! All that people have they will give to save their lives. ⁵ But stretch out your hand now and touch his bone and his flesh, and he will curse you to your face." ⁶ The LORD said to Satan," Very well, he is in your power; only spare his life."

⁷ So Satan went out from the presence of the LORD, and inflicted loathsome sores on Job from the sole of his foot to the crown of his head. ⁸ Job took a potsherd with which to scrape himself and sat among the ashes.

⁹ Then his wife said to him, "Do you still persist in your integrity? Curse God and die." ¹⁰ But he said to her, "You speak as any foolish woman would speak. Shall we receive the good at the hand of God, and not receive the bad?" In all this Job did not sin with his lips.

It begins like a nursery rhyme. "There once was a man from the land of Uz." We don't know where "Uz" is. It almost sounds made-up. It is a place though... or was a place. We can imagine it to be any place, even our own place, our own town. That is the beauty of a nursery rhyme. It also sounds like a riddle. "There once was a man from the land of Uz who never did anything wrong." You've read riddles like this. "Never did anything wrong?" That's the hook!   You know something is about to happen, something to test the man who never did anything wrong. It is a perfect riddle. It is the perfect nursery rhyme. Only this is no nursery rhyme. There is something much deeper going on here than Humpty Dumpty. Job is an unsettling, disturbing read.[1]

One needs some resources to help navigate Job. I often go to the Barton College library when I need extra resources that I can't find in my tired collection. They have a tremendous religious and theological section. The folks there are enormously friendly and helpful. "Have a nice day," I'm told when I check out. "Thanks for coming by." Last week, the man promptly checked me out and said, "Happy Reading!" Well, it is Job, so.... I'm not so sure how happy this will be.

Job is like a nursery rhyme, but it isn't. Job is an ancient folk tale that has a long shelf life. Job is a wonderful read, if it is still disturbing. The first thing most folks struggle with is the role of God and Satan. The two essentially place a wager on Job's life. "How much do you think Job will take before he breaks?" "I say a lot!" "I say a little!" Then God lets Satan unleash a world of hurt upon poor Job. That is what happens. It seems harsh. It seems cruel. I will tell you, though, that this is not the definitive statement on how God relates to humanity. This is not the fully developed theology on how evil makes its way in the world. There is more the Bible will say on those things. This is one story. This is a folktale, an ancient story, drawn from the culture around it and included in our Scriptures. It is included in the canon of our Scripture, not because of some historical connection to Israel and not because it answers the reason for suffering. In fact, it creates more questions than answers in that regard. It was included in the canon of Scripture because of the weighty matters of its content, because any faith in God will necessarily suffer with the question of suffering and the Bible is unafraid to wrestle with that topic to its very depths. The story begins with these talks between God and Satan only as a way to get to a larger matter. The issue for the writer is not, why would God do such a thing to someone he cares for. No, the issue is

---

[1]Resources include Norman C. Habel, *Job: Knox Preaching Guides.* (Richmond: John Knox Press, 1981).

David Bartlett and Barbara Brown Taylor, ed. Feasting on the Word (Louisville: WJKP, 2009).

Marvin H. Pope. The Anchor Bible: Job. (Garden City, NY: Doubleday Press, 1961).

why would, why *should* Job ever concern himself with God to begin with?

Lets' review the story. Satan and God strike up a conversation. "Have you ever noticed my servant Job? There is no one like him! He persists in integrity!" Satan snorts, "Please! "Do you think Job worships you for no reason? Look at him! He is set-up pretty well - 7,000 sheep, 3,000 camels, 500 oxen, 500 donkeys, a home, a wife, 7 sons, 3 daughters and a slew of servants. Of course he likes God! Take it all away, and you will see what happens. He will curse you to your face." "You're on!" says God. With that it all starts falling apart for Job. First his oxen get stolen. Then his donkeys. Then his sheep die in an horrific fire. Then his camels are stolen. Then his servants are killed. He is ruined. He has lost everything. Then his house collapses, killing all this child. It is a tragedy. Job is understandably grieved. Yet, he never abandons faith. In all this, Scripture says, "He did not sin by charging God with some wrongdoing."

Satan, though, is persistent. He returns to the Lord, and the story repeats itself, almost verbatim. Again they barter. "Did you see Job? There is no one like him! He persists in his integrity, even after all the stuff you did to him." Satan snorts, "Please! All that a person has he will give to save his hide. Let me go after his flesh and bone, and he'll started singing a different tune." So it then gets even worse for Job - loathsome sores, pain, suffering. Now, wounded, weary and without hope, Job is suffering. Job is suffering body, mind and soul. And it all happened in a blink of an eye. In just a few verses, he has lost everything. Job now sits among "the ashes, "which could be the ashes of his crumbled house and life. It could also be, some scholars believe, this section of town where people dump their garbage. His life is literally now a dumpster fire. In any case, he lost it all...in the blink of an eye.

His wife asks a question. "Why do you still persist with this? Curse God and die!" Now, people over the generations have given her a hard time. You do realize, though, that she has suffered too, right? Her life is changed. Her loss is deep. Her suffering is real. Her economic security is gone. Her children are under that pill of rubble. She suffers too. She has a different reaction though. She has a *normal* reaction. She has a logical, reasonable reaction. She has an honest reaction. Why *shouldn't* Job give up the ghost on this? I mean, what good is his faith doing him at this point? Curse God and die! Curse God and be done with it. What else can God do that God hasn't already been done to Job? Kill him? That would be a blessing! Oh no. The wife is the only one making any sense here. This all points back the first question, the most important question in this reading. "Come on God, do think Job fears you for no reason?" Put it another way. Does Job only serve God for the blessings?

You have likely heard of the "Health and Wealth Gospel." It is very common these days, probably the most common gospel these days, preached all over the place, by well-intentioned preachers, particularly here in America. It is the whole notion that God wants you rich and successful, and if you do right, you will be. It is actually a very old gospel, older than Jesus even. It keeps getting regenerated, usually in times of moral uncertainty. People flock to it now. Curiously, in this scripture, its main proponent is Satan.

There is a problem with the Health and Wealth Gospel, though. If evidence of God is the abundance of your blessings, then when those blessings are gone, you have no God. More specifically, the problem is that you have made God into a vending machine. Sadly, it is common gospel. It is very common for a people who see themselves at the center of the universe and have no use for anything that does not or anyone who will not give them something they want.

James Gustafson is a well-respected Christian ethicist. He has written about the contrast between a utilitarian faith and a theo-centric one.[2] The former justifies religious faith by its benefits - what does one "get out of it." How does it serve me? It is very straight-forward. It is how we buy everything from cars to paper towels. It is often how we enter into relationships. It is very clear, if also a little shallow. It is utilitarian. On the other hand, a theo-centric faith focuses on a serving God and God's purposes beyond whatever might or might not be received by the believer. One isn't the center of the universe in this model. One's

---

[2] James M. Gustafson, Ethics from a Theocentric Perspective. (Chicago: Univ of Chicago Press, 1981).

life and possessions are not. Even one's eternal salvation is not the most important thing. In this kind of faith, in this mature faith, all those matters are left to God. It is hard to actually think that way, believe that way or be that way. Yet, there sure is some peace in that way.

No one wants to visit the land of Uz. No one wants to be in that kind of suffering and loss. Who would? There is something wrong with the person who would! And so, it only makes sense that we would do our own bartering, that we would seek a God who keeps us out of Uz, that we would dump every coin we have into that holy vending machine just to keep the good things coming. But that isn't the world we live in, is it? Not in reality. God has not created a world that is free of suffering. The reality is that in this world there is both suffering and there is respite. There is both. Ultimately, what God appreciates about Job is not that Job is good or pure in our sense of things, but that he is never turns away from God.

I know people who have been in this land of Uz, who have been to the place where they about lost it all. You might be one of them. It is a terrible place. Some people who end up in Uz lose their faith. Who can blame them? At the same time, I've also known a few who landed in Uz and held on to that faith, held on to it as if it was a life raft, the only thing keeping them afloat, the only thing keeping them from drifting away into the abyss.

That famous 20th century writer and theologian CS Lewis wrote a little book called *The Screwtape Letters*. It is a folktale itself, one that also attempts to point to a deeper truth. In it, CS Lewis records the advice of a senior devil, Screwtape, to his nephew, Wormwood, who is trying to undo the faith of a recently converted Christian. At one point, Screwtape says to his nephew, "Our cause is never more in danger than when a human, no longer desiring, but still intending to do God's work, looks around the universe from which every trace of God seems to have vanished and asks why he has been forsaken and still obeys."[3] One cannot read the first part of Job and not ask "why do I believe?" Is faith a commodity to me? What would happen if it didn't pay off? Worse, what would happen if it went the other way? We are generally

---

[3] C.S. Lewis, The Screwtape Letters (New York: Collier Books, 1961).

concerned with our happiness. Conversely, God is generally concerned with our faithfulness. In truth, those do not have to be mutually exclusive. That God is interested in our faithfulness is simply another way of saying that God is first and foremost interested in our relationship.

What we ultimately know about how God deals with people is not the story of Job, but the story of Jesus. Everything in Scripture is read through that window, through the lens of that relationship. Suffering is not removed in a life of faith, but neither is it unaccompanied and neither is it unresolved. God does not leave us to our own devices. God gives himself to the suffering of the world, to the suffering in the world, so that we might be redeemed through it. God does not dispense hardship at Satan's bidding, any more than God dispenses goodies when we drop in enough coins. Suffering is part of life. Peace comes not from avoiding it, but in knowing the God who abides with you through it.

Thanks be to God.

Then Job Opened His Mouth
Job 3:1-10, 23:1-9

After this Job opened his mouth and cursed the day of his birth. *²Job said:*

³" Let the day perish in which I was born, and the night that said, 'A man-child is conceived.' ⁴Let that day be darkness! May God above not seek it, or light shine on it. ⁵Let gloom and deep darkness claim it. Let clouds settle upon it; let the blackness of the day terrify it. ⁶That night—let thick darkness seize it! Let it not rejoice among the days of the year; let it not come into the number of the months. ⁷Yes, let that night be barren; let no joyful cry be heard in it. ⁸Let those curses it who curse the Sea, those who are skilled to rouse up Leviathan. ⁹Let the stars of its dawn be dark; let it hope for light but have none; may it not see the eyelids of the morning— ¹⁰because it did not shut the doors of my mother's womb and hide trouble from my eyes.

Then Job answered: *²"Today also my complaint is bitter; his hand is heavy despite my groaning. ³Oh, that I knew where I might find him, that I might come even to his dwelling! ⁴I would lay my case before him and fill my mouth with arguments. ⁵I would learn what he would answer me and understand what he would say to me. ⁶Would he contend with me in the greatness of his power? No; but he would give heed to me. ⁷There an upright person could reason with him, and I should be acquitted forever by my judge. ⁸"If I go forward, he is not there; or backward, I cannot perceive him; ⁹on the left he hides, and I cannot behold him; I turn to the right, but I cannot see him.*

Not all losses are created equal. Some funerals, some visitations are far more difficult than others. This isn't saying a certain loss is less significant to a family or to you. Circumstances make a difference. Some funerals, some visitations move along with a sad predictability. Other visitations... well, you just don't know what to say. Have you ever you ever been in a situation so grim, so tragic, that you didn't know what to say? After you have been in those moments often enough, you realize, that often there is nothing to say. That is what happens here in Job ...at least initially.

Job has suffered great loss. And because he is grieving, his friends are grieving. They grieve for him and with him. In one of the more poignant scenes in all the Old Testament, the friends come and sit with him.

> *"They sat with him on the ground seven days and seven nights,*
> *and no one spoke a word to him,*
> *for they saw that his suffering was very great."*

They didn't speak at first. They just sat with him.

In 1983 a friend of mine died in a lacrosse accident at the University of Virginia. The visitation and funeral, as you imagine, was bleak affair. I remember it well. His whole family was there, of course. Mother, father, and three brothers, the youngest being 12, all lined up in the visitation line. What do you say to a 12-year-old? The 12-year-old's friend knew. Tommy stood next to Grier all night. He never said a word, but he stood by his side the duration of the visitation. He never left his side. He just stood there with him in silence. This was a great lesson. When you do not know what to do, you just go. If there is nothing to say, you just go and be. The church has done this for centuries. This is what happens in Job... at least initially.

Now, if you recall, Satan had a wager. He felt sure that when faced with the loss of all his life, Job would curse God to his face. Yet after the loss of his home, his income and even after the loss of his children, Job remained strong. He did not "charge God with any wrongdoing." So, if you recall, Satan increased the pressure. Certainly, in the face of physical suffering, Job would break and would curse God to God's face. Yet, after Job is inflicted with some great and terrible disease, Job... remained strong. After this second round of tragedy, Job never says anything bad. But he thinks it.

You can see for yourself. Compare Job's reactions at the end of chapter 1 and the end of chapter 2. At the end of the first round, Job worships God, offers a gracious theological perspective about his predicament. At the end of chapter 2, after the second round of tragedy, the only thing reported about Job's reaction is that "he didn't sin with his lips." That is far different than what was reported earlier.[4]

Job is now silent. Job is silent, but in my mind, Job is stewing. Job stews for seven days and seven nights. His friends come and stay with him, in silence. But after seven days, Job is ready to talk. After abiding in his dignity and uprightness for seven days, Job has something to say. Now, after seven days of sitting with all this loss which he did not deserve, Job opens his mouth. This is exactly how the scripture describes it, by the way. "And then Job opened his mouth." Job finally opens his mouth and out comes a torrent of anger, defensiveness and rage. It is a category 5 on an unsuspecting beach town. It is awesome.

His friends are predictably blown away. They didn't see this coming. They are surprised. They are also now filled with advice and counsel. "You shouldn't say that! That isn't any way to talk! You are going to regret speaking like this!" These friends begin arguing with him because they have some of their own thoughts they've been sitting on. "People get what they deserve, so you must have done something to deserve this. What are you not telling us? You ought to come clean. There must be some moral failure on your part. There is some theological naiveté on your part. You don't know what you are talking about." These friends and Job get into an argument. Back and forth it goes, for chapter upon chapter.

Scholars have tried to categorize Job's speech to some literary form. Is it prose? Is it poetry? Is it an ancient Hebrew style of lament? But there is no category for "rant." This isn't to say, though, that Job's word are not calculated. Look closely. The first thing Job does is curse the day of his birth. That is the first thing he says. "Job opens his mouth and cursed the day of his birth." He wishes he had never been born. This is sad. It is also significant. Earlier in the story, when Satan was seeking to destroy Job, do you recall the one thing that God put a

---

[4] Resources: Norman C. Habel, Job: Knox Preaching Guides. (Richmond: John Knox Press, 1981).

David Bartlett and Barbara Brown Taylor, ed. Feasting on the Word (Louisville: WJKP, 2009).

Marvin H. Pope. The Anchor Bible: Job. (Garden City, NY: Doubleday Press, 1961).

hedge around, the one thing that God said Satan could not touch? Job's life. Satan couldn't touch his life. "You can take away all kinds of stuff, but you cannot touch his life. Life is mine. I give it. I get to take it. Life is precious. Life is valuable. Lift is a gift. Life is the best thing I have for Job and the one thing I will keep for him." This is very Biblical, by the way. God has always, will always, be for life. When Job finally speaks, though, the first thing he says is "I hate my life and wish I was never born." That is pointed.

Let's say one day your father pulls you aside and tells you what he has left for you in his will. He comes to you and says, "I have divided up my possessions, my treasures. There are many good things, but for you I have saved my prized beach house. I love that beach house. I have great memories there. Of all the good things, it is the most cherished, and I want you to have it." You then immediately turn to a friend, "You know, I hate that beach house. It is a hot, sticky, smelly dump. I wouldn't care if that house got washed into the sea." This is what Job does. This is meant to hurt.

The wager was that Job would curse God to his face. And Job doesn't do that. He doesn't. So, good for him. He held the line. Instead, he sits on his words for seven days and then he curses God's most treasured gift to him. And he is just getting started.

Did you hear what Job said in Chapter 23? The most repeated affirmations of God in the Old Testament are that God is merciful and steadfast, merciful and steadfast, merciful and steadfast. Here, Job debunks both of those.

> *"Despite my groaning, God's hand is still on me, holding me down."*
> *God, thus, is not merciful.*
> *"If I could find him, I might offer my complaints directly to him.*
> *But I can't find him. God is not here."*
> *God, thus, is not steadfast.*
> *"If I go forward, he is not there; or backward, I cannot perceive him;*
> *If I turn left, he hides, and I cannot behold him;*
> *I turn to the right, but I cannot see him either."*

God is not here. God is nowhere to be found. God is not present or available or abiding or steadfast. God is not with us. God does not go with us. God is gone. Compare this to Psalm 139. The contrast is shocking. There may not be another more vicious, more personal attack on God ever. No, he doesn't curse God, but wow, this sure seems worse to me. It seems personal.

I've known people who take certain comments extremely personal. They seem overly sensitive. You tell them, "You don't have to take it so personal!" They tell you, "I can't help it. It IS personal to me!" Some things we do not take as personal. "Tom, that road in front of your house is a mess. There is no curb, the paving is breaking away and potholes are everywhere. It's awful." That doesn't bother me. That isn't my problem. I can discuss it without emotion. Other things I might take more personal, other things in which I am invested, other things for which I have bled.

Job is reacting rather strongly. Job is rather harsh. You might say Job is over-the-top in his response and has crossed the line. Job is taking all this rather personally. Maybe so, but I think it is a good thing. This is personal to Job. This is personal to Job because his relationship with God is personal.

Sometimes we walk through life with a Victorian-styled faith, overly concerned about how it looks or how it sounds, making sure we bow when we should and curtsy when appropriate, being more interested in looking really nice than being real. Sometimes we walk through life with a Puritanical-styled faith, keeping our emotions in check, taking the bad with the good without protest.

"Thy will be done," is what we are taught to pray and rightly so. Sometimes, though, a "Thy will be done" attitude is just an excuse for laziness. Sometimes a "Thy will be done" manner is a laisse-faire faith that really isn't faith at all. It is disconnected, fake and anemic. Say what you want about Job, but Job is not disconnected. Job is not fake, and Job is not anemic. Job is invested. Job has lost everything. He will not lose God! He might be harsh. He might be rude. He might be over-the-top, but he is not indifferent.

In the first verse of Chapter 1 of this book, the scripture says that Job feared God. John Calvin distinguished between two types of fear: servile fear and proper fear. Servile fear is fear of some wrath, fear that God is "going to get you," Proper fear is fear of loss, fear of offending or wounding the other, fear of disappointing the other, fear of disconnecting with the other. Ultimately, servile fear is fear for oneself. The other is a fear of reverence and respect. Job feared God. He didn't fear what God would do to him. What more could happen to him that hadn't already happened? No, Job feared the loss of God, the only thing he had left.

In the face of tragedy, we are often told there are two choices. Be meek and mild and take what comes or give up the faith and any notion of a God who cares or loves. Job offers another way, a third way. He will not give up his faith nor will he give up his voice. And in doing so, Job stands in the company of a whole list of Biblical figures who boldly do the same.

The first verse of the first chapter of this book says, very plainly, that Job is righteous. He is blameless and upright. If I take that seriously, in light of the rest of the book of Job, then righteousness isn't simply about how pure I am before God, but how honest I am before God. Sometimes we don't know what to say, to each other, to God, and sometimes silence is the best thing. Still, just is there is a time for silence, there is also a time for speech, and our willingness to utter the hard thing, or hear a friend utter the hard thing, is, believe it or not, an act of righteousness. It is an act of faith.

Thanks be to God.

Out of a Whirlwind

Job 38: 1-21; 40:7-14

Then the LORD *answered Job out of the whirlwind:*

²"Who is this that darkens counsel by words without knowledge? ³Gird up your loins like a man, I will question you, and you shall declare to me. ⁴"Where were you when I laid the foundation of the earth? Tell me, if you have understanding. ⁵Who determined its measurements—surely you know! Or who stretched the line upon it? ⁶On what were its bases sunk, or who laid its cornerstone ⁷when the morning stars sang together, and all the heavenly beings shouted for joy? ⁸"Or who shut in the sea with doors when it burst out from the womb?— ⁹when I made the clouds its garment, and thick darkness its swaddling band, ¹⁰and prescribed bounds for it, and set bars and doors, ¹¹and said, 'Thus far shall you come, and no farther, and here shall your proud waves be stopped'? ¹²"Have you commanded the morning since your days began, and caused the dawn to know its place, ¹³so that it might take hold of the skirts of the earth, and the wicked be shaken out of it? ¹⁴It is changed like clay under the seal, and it is dyed like a garment. ¹⁵Light is withheld from the wicked, and their uplifted arm is broken. ¹⁶"Have you entered into the springs of the sea, or walked in the recesses of the deep? ¹⁷Have the gates of death been revealed to you, or have you seen the gates of deep darkness? ¹⁸Have you comprehended the expanse of the earth? Declare, if you know all this. ¹⁹"Where is the way to the dwelling of light, and where is the place of darkness, ²⁰that you may take it to its territory and that you may discern the paths to its home? ²¹Surely you know, for you were born then, and the number of your days is great!

⁷"Gird up your loins like a man; I will question you, and you declare to me. ⁸Will you even put me in the wrong? Will you condemn me that you may be justified? ⁹Have you an arm like God, and can you thunder with a voice like his? ¹⁰"Deck yourself with majesty and dignity; clothe yourself with glory and splendor. ¹¹Pour out the overflowings of your anger, and look on all who are proud, and abase them. ¹²Look on all who are proud and bring them low; tread down the wicked where they stand.

¹³Hide them all in the dust together; bind their faces in the world below. ¹⁴Then I will also acknowledge to you that your own right hand can give you victory.

They say to be careful what you wish for. They should have said that to Job. Job had some wishes. "If I had my way, I would defend my ways to his face. Oh, that I knew where I might find him, I would bring my case before him. I would fill my mouth with arguments. I would teach and he would answer me. But if I go forward, he is not there. If I go backward, I cannot perceive him. If I turn left, he hides, and I cannot behold him. I turn to the right, but I cannot see him either." Job wanted God. Well, here in Chapter 38, Job now gets a full measure of God, and it is a rather unhappy measure at that!

You might recall that Job, as the story begins, is minding his own business. Then, through some sort of wager between God and Satan as to Job's faithful fortitude, Job is burdened with enormous suffering. Job, scripture reports, is a righteous man. He is a good man, a faithful man and an innocent man. Nonetheless, through forces greater than him and beyond his understanding, he suddenly endures terrible hardship. Like many people in such a situation, he wants to know why. He has three friends, three who are kind of enough to come and ponder with him, to suffer with him. Yet their rhetoric brings more questions than answers, for they are sure Job must have done something to deserve all this hardship. After days of silent suffering, Job explodes in a torrent of anger and blame. With each "suggestion" of his friends, Job's anger only seems to increase. Essentially, "I have done nothing wrong," he would say. "God has some explaining to do. This is not the way it should be. This is not the way life should go. I am not the one who is failing. God either is sleeping on the job or is not doing it very well."

Yet if Job is rather forceful in his fury, rather pointed in his accusations, rather sharp with his speech, then God puts him to shame. For it is now God's turn to speak. "Who is this that darkens counsel by words without knowledge?" [You don't know what you are talking about.] "Gird up your loins like a man!" [You want to be tough? Get ready!] "I will question you, and you shall declare to me." [You have questions? Great. Now I have some questions of you!] And with that God unleashes about sixty relentless questions on Job. "Where were you when...? Who do you think you are that...? Can you...? Did you...? How might you...?" And on and on it goes. It is said that no one dares speak to God as boldly as Job. That may be true, but I cannot recall God unleashing on anyone as intensely as God does on Job.

> *"Where were you when I laid the foundation of the earth?*
> *Tell me, if you have understanding.*
> *Who determined its measurements?*
> *Surely you know!*
> *Have you commanded the morning since your days began,*
> *and caused the dawn to know its place,*
> *so that it might take hold of the skirts of the earth,*
> *and the wicked be shaken out of it?*
> *Have you entered into the springs of the sea,*
> *or walked in the recesses of the deep?*
> *Have the gates of death been revealed to you,*
> *or have you seen the gates of deep darkness?*
> *Have you comprehended the expanse of the earth?*
> *Declare, if you know all this!*
> *Where is the way to the dwelling of light,*
> *and where is the place of darkness,*
> *that you may take it to its territory*
> *and that you may discern the paths to its home?*
> *Surely you know, for you were born then,*
> *and the number of your days is great!*

Whatever Job uttered in ferocity, God matches it, in duration, volume, intensity and sarcasm. There is nothing like this anywhere.

In all this, though, there is one disconnect between the two, between Job's rants and God's. There is a disconnect. If you spent enough time in the book, you will notice it. Job's questions never get answered. For all God's speech, for all God's rhetoric, God never answers Job's questions.

Now, God does answer Job. In fact that is the first verse of Chapter 38, "God answered Job out of a whirlwind." So God answers Job, but God never answers Job's *question*. Through it all, God never answers the question, "Why do I suffer?" That is Job's question. And honestly, that is THE question, is it not? "Why do I suffer?" There are other questions. There are many questions. "How might my sins be forgiven? How do I live in faith? How do I grow to God? Who is my neighbor? What must I do to inherit eternal life?" All good, Biblical questions will long shelf-lives. But, in all candor, there is but one question that people most often ask. And it isn't about sin - though it might should be. And it isn't about eternal life -though it well could be. It is about suffering. Why do the innocent suffer? It is a fair question. It is an understandable question, for Job or anyone in a Job-like moment. And so it is fair that Job wants an answer. But he does not get it.

God speaks for three chapters. Never answers it. God says lots of things. God speaks of the expanse of the universe. God speaks of the details of all these bizarre creatures. God speaks of power and wonder, of height and depth of creation. God says so much, but God never answers the questions of suffering. God doesn't address why Job suffers. God doesn't answer why anyone suffers. God doesn't even talk about suffering at all. God doesn't bring up the word suffering or hardship or peril or trouble or bum luck or bad hair days. God doesn't talk about why bad things happen to good people or why good things happen to bad people. For that matter, God doesn't talk about why bad things happen to bad people or good things to good people! God says so much, but God never answers the question of suffering, at least not in a way we would think. What God does, though, is frame the question. What God does is take Job on a trip.

One of the greatest blessings my parents gave me was travel. They would take us places. I'm not talking necessarily about grand, far-away places like Paris, but distant places, nonetheless. They would take us from the city to the country. They would take us to the beach or to the mountains. They would take us out of state, to Miami or to Maine, to DC and then to Daytona, to New York then to New Mexico, to eat crab cakes in Baltimore and buffalo in Boulder. Such ventures have the benefit of reshaping your world view. We would see people in other lives. "They eat this food? They live in this weather? They do this kind of job? They sleep in this house?" Suddenly, we would look upon our world a little differently. Mark Twain said once that "travel is fatal to prejudice, bigotry and narrow-mindedness." Gustave Flaubert said that "travel makes one modest, you see what a tiny place you occupy in the world."

This is what God does here. God does not so much come to Job and sit with him on the ash heap, as God picks him and takes him on a trip, and in doing so, Job sees the world a little differently. God shows Job creation - from sun to sea, from mountain to valley, from light to darkness. God picks out creatures and dissects them. God points to features and describes them. God demonstrates the wonder of the world, the complicated relationships and the power behind it all. Now this is not to dismiss Job's suffering. It is not to deny the hardship, the pain or the struggle. It is only to see it from another plane. And in doing so, Job's sufferings are now seen as part of a vast expanse of things, far too transcendent for any mere mortal to comprehend. Walter Brueggemann says that "For all his persistence, Job cannot finally extricate himself from the limitations of his own creature-liness."[5] God's speech allows him to do so.

When it comes to suffering, everyone wants to know "why," as if by knowing "why" we might gain a better control of the madness. Job spent thirty-seven chapters asking why. Then, God responds. God responds not in direct response to Job's why, but in a tour of the grandeur, beauty and order of creation. If asking "why" is a feeble human attempt to get control of life, then God's response could give one even less sense of control. Ultimately, it forces one to consider a force beyond one's control.

William Sloan Coffin, a renowned preacher, tells a story of a tragic loss in his youth. When he was an undergraduate student at Yale, three of his friends were killed in a car accident after the driver fell asleep at the wheel. At the funeral, Coffin was sickened by the piety of a priest as he spoke the words from the Book of Job: "The Lord gave, and the Lord has taken away; blessed be the name of the Lord." Coffin was so outraged that he considered tripping the priest as he processed back down the aisle of the church. As he was preparing to do so, a small voice asked him, "what part of the phrase are you objecting to?" He says that he thought it was the second part, the "taken away" part. Then it dawned on him. "No. I was protesting the first part, 'the Lord gave' part. "It hit me hard that it was not my world, that at best we

---

[5] Walter Brueggemann, Charles Cousar, Beverly Gaventa, James Newsome, <u>Text for Preaching: Lectionary Commentary Based on NRSV, Year B</u> (Louisville: WJKP, 1993).

were all guests. And 'the Lord gave' is a statement against which all the spears of human pride have to be hurled and shattered."[6] We are a small part of a big world. That is not to dismiss the suffering, but to see it from another view and to associate it with the suffering of others, of even God's suffering with the world.

Job, at last, is granted an audience with God. The God who seemed so elusive before is very present now, maybe more than Job wanted. Job, of course, is not prepared for this conversation for the simple reason that Job has consistently underestimated God.

In truth, God did answer Job. It may not have been as Job would have expected. It may not have been when Job would have liked. It may not have been how Job would have wanted. Nonetheless, God did answer. Job's friends are sure that Job sinned, and therefore he has been abandoned by God. Job argues that he has not sinned, and thus he is undeservedly abandoned. What they have in common is that they are all so sure that Job is cut-off from God and his suffering is evidence of it. But that is not true. That is where everyone in the story is so wrong. One cannot deny Job's suffering. Job knows himself. What he does not fully comprehend is God. Suffering is not a sign of God's abandonment. In fact, it is often the vehicle for God's presence! You will note that in this story the only time Job ever experiences God is *during* his suffering.

People come to the book of Job expecting an answer to the question so suffering. Job comes to the Book of Job expecting an answer to the question of suffering. Sadly, the answer does not come as we might like. In fact, as is literally the case with Job, we often come away from the conversation with more questions given to us than answers provided. Still, from a bird's eye view, after a tour of the expanse of God's speech, the scripture does offer a rather straightforward answer, an answer, in the words of one theologian, "as remarkable for what it omits as for what it contains." Essentially, you, me, Job simply do not possess the wisdom to contest the Almighty. It is far better to trust God and be at peace.

Amen.

---

[6] William Sloan Coffin, <u>Letters to a Young Doubter</u> (Louisville: WJKP, 1985).

After the Whirlwind
Job 42: 1-17

Then Job answered the LORD:

*² "I know that you can do all things, and that no purpose of yours can be thwarted.
³ 'Who is this that hides counsel without knowledge?' Therefore I have uttered what
I did not understand, things too wonderful for me, which I did not know. ⁴ 'Hear,
and I will speak; I will question you, and you declare to me.' ⁵ I had heard of you
by the hearing of the ear, but now my eye sees you; ⁶ therefore I despise myself, and
repent in dust and ashes."*

*⁷ After the LORD had spoken these words to Job, the LORD said to Eliphaz the
Temanite: "My wrath is kindled against you and against your two friends; for you
have not spoken of me what is right, as my servant Job has. ⁸ Now therefore take
seven bulls and seven rams, and go to my servant Job, and offer up for yourselves a
burnt offering; and my servant Job shall pray for you, for I will accept his prayer
not to deal with you according to your folly; for you have not spoken of me what is
right, as my servant Job has done." ⁹ So Eliphaz the Temanite and Bildad the
Shuhite and Zophar the Naamathite went and did what the LORD had told them;
and the LORD accepted Job's prayer.*

*¹⁰ And the LORD restored the fortunes of Job when he had prayed for his friends;
and the LORD gave Job twice as much as he had before. ¹¹ Then there came to him
all his brothers and sisters and all who had known him before, and they ate bread
with him in his house; they showed him sympathy and comforted him for all the evil
that the LORD had brought upon him; and each of them gave him a piece of
money and a gold ring. ¹² The LORD blessed the latter days of Job more than his
beginning; and he had fourteen thousand sheep, six thousand camels, a thousand
yoke of oxen, and a thousand donkeys. ¹³ He also had seven sons and three
daughters. ¹⁴ He named the first Jemimah, the second Keziah, and the third Keren-
happuch. ¹⁵ In all the land there were no women so beautiful as Job's daughters; and
their father gave them an inheritance along with their brothers. ¹⁶ After this Job
lived one hundred and forty years, and saw his children, and his children's children,
four generations. ¹⁷ And Job died, old and full of days.*

So God restored everything. After God let it all evaporate into a pile
of dust and ashes, God put it all back. After Job lost and lost it all
- his fortune, his economy, his children, his home, his life, his health -

and after Job suffered and wailed against God, and after God wailed against Job a little bit too, after the dust settled and everyone made peace, God just put it all back. Like it never happened. God restored his fortunes. That is the first thing the Scripture says. God gave him twice as much as he had before - 14,000 sheep, instead of 7,000 sheep, 6,000 camels instead of 3,000 camels, 1000 yoke of oxen instead of 500 yoke, 1000 donkeys instead of 500 donkeys. He didn't double-up on children, but he did get 10 to replace the 10 lost - 7 sons and 3 daughters, just like before. Also, all his friends and family, brothers and sisters, returned. After his fortunes were restored, they all showed back up, and showering him sympathy and concern...and money. Each brought him some money, as a nice gift. Everything went back to normal. It was just great. It is a perfect ending ... I guess.

I just wonder though ... is it really the same? Is it really better? Hurricanes blow through North Carolina every season and leave a mess. After the storm, it can be beautiful in the sky, but down on the ground there is a mess to pick up. I've heard people after a hurricane destroys their home and lives. They rebuild, but it is never the same. They might have insurance and can put it all back together again, but they aren't the same afterward, are they? If a hurricane blew away El's Burger Stand in Morehead City, the owners couldn't just rebuild the exact same place. It wouldn't be the same, would it?

I know Job has a lot more stuff now, twice as much stuff. That is really nice. Now all his friends just happen to show up again, now that he has money. They bring him more money. For some reason, I just wonder if he wants it, if it means as much to him as it once did. And, yes, he has ten new children to replace the children he lost. But, from what I understand and from what I can only fear to imagine, you don't exactly replace children, do you? So I guess, I imagine that this restoration is not quite so seamless. I just wonder.

Job has just survived a storm, a whirlwind, the flood of devastation in the loss of all he had, the eruption of his own emotional volcano, and then a whirlwind of God's epic response. If you recall, after days of silent suffering, Job then explodes in a torrent of anger. His friends try to corral him in, try to get him to confess to whatever wrong he has done, for surely, he had done something awful to receive all this awful suffering. His friends so sure in their orthodoxy. His friends are so consistent in their judgment. His friends are so unwavering in their theology. But Job is immovable. He is insistent and incensed. "I have done nothing wrong. God has some explaining to do. This is not the way it should be. This is not the way life should go. I am not the one who is failing." Job demands to be heard. But so does God, and God then unleashes God's own venting, and quickly puts Job in his place. "Who is this that darkens counsel by words without knowledge?" And with that God unleashes about sixty relentless questions, on Job. "Where were you when...? Who do you think you are that...? Can you...? Did you...? How might you...?" And on and on and on it goes.

If Job's laments are a storm surge, then God's speech is tropical force winds. Today, though, is the calm after the storm. Chapter 42. Job seemingly relents, and God apparently blesses him for it. And if the scripture ended there and our study delved no deeper, the story would end very neatly. [Job had trouble. Job talked back to God. God put him in his place. Job said he was sorry. Job learned his little lesson. And that would be that.] But that is not what happens. That is often how we sum up the uncomfortable story of Job, but that is not what happens. And thank goodness that is not what happens, because it would be a shame if it did. Because the suffering, the real suffering needs a response, even if it doesn't get an answer, it needs a response.

You do know that there is a lot of talk about whether this story is true or not.[7] Most scholars think it is not a 'true' story, in the sense that there was really a Job and it really happened. Of course, more conservative ones insist it is a 'true' story because it is in the Bible. Both miss this point completely. It doesn't matter if the story really happened. What matters is that the story of Job is in our Bible, and therefore there is something here that God is teaching us. What matters is that the story is real. It is real because suffering is real. Whether or not there was really a Job makes no difference because

---

[7] Resources: Norman C. Habel, Job: Knox Preaching Guides. (Richmond: John Knox Press, 1981). David Bartlett and Barbara Brown Taylor, ed. Feasting on the Word (Louisville: WJKP, 2009). Marvin H. Pope. The Anchor Bible: Job. (Garden City, NY: Doubleday Press, 1961).

there is a Job somewhere today. There is always a Job and that is the problem! There is always a Job because there is always suffering and even if it doesn't get an answer in this book, suffering deserves a response. And, thank heavens, we get one, even if the notion of orthodox theology is lost.

Verse 7. It is one of the most stunning verses in Scripture. It is the rallying cry of every unjust sufferer. After Job says his words, the Lord speaks.

> *7 After the LORD had spoken these words to Job, the LORD said to Eliphaz the Temanite: "My wrath is kindled against you and against your two friends; for you have not spoken of me what is right, as my servant Job has.*

Did you hear that? Did you hear what God says to Job's pious friends? Scripture records it twice, so we do not miss it.

"You have not spoken of me what is right, as my servant Job has."

They were wrong. Job was right. Well, I thought Job was wrong? I thought Job spoke incorrectly? Apparently not. Job, apparently, spoke what was true. So what's the difference? What was the difference between what friends said and what Job said? Well, the friends spoke about God. Job spoke *to* God. The friends spoke with judgment. Job spoke of confession and defiance. The friends spoke of this system where the good get good and the bad and get bad. Job spoke of injustice. The friends spoke about order and orthodoxy. Job spoke of his truth. The friends spoke with certitude. Job spoke with doubt and candor.

In our effort to be religious, in our attempts to be faithful even, we are often prone to think we know more than we do. It is like that expression that a little bit of knowledge is a dangerous thing. Too often our views of God become cemented in a religious certitude that, in the end, dismisses the humanity of our neighbors and the divinity of our God. We become too quick to hush an inappropriate remark, to put our finger to our mouth, "Oh, you shouldn't say that! Don't speak that way!" We become too quick to correct, "No, no. You must not say that. No, no." When we do it to others or ourselves, it is oppressive and unfaithful.

One scholar says that Job's bold assertions are closer to what is right than all his friends wise and orthodox theology. And if Job is humbled in God's response, then the friends are humiliated. In the end, it is Job who is called to pray for them.[8] Maybe Job is over-the-top at times, maybe he is rather demonstrative, maybe he questions God's wisdom, God's timing and God's ways. Nonetheless, Job never, ever denies God.

Of course Job is right. We are told from the beginning that he is righteous. Moreover, at closer view, Job's repentance is not what we often think it is. After God unleashed on Job, Job is taken back. And two of God's myriad of responses still ring in Job's ear. Job repeats them:

> *"Who is this that hides counsel without knowledge?"*
> *"Hear and I will speak, and I will question you."*

To these questions, Job affirms the awesomeness of God. Job attests that there is a broadness to God, a mystery and wonder of God beyond his comprehension. Job confesses a new understanding of God, where before he knew God by what people told him, now he knows God because of what he has seen. Job repents, but he never repents from his hard feelings. Job does not express sorrow over sin or remorse over guilt. He does not confess that he was overly self-righteous. He does not retract his assertion about unjust treatment. Job's repentance, his change, is a deeper wisdom and a deeper faith. It is a change of attitude, an acknowledgement that there are levels of divine mystery and might which he cannot grasp. It is a more expansive faith. It is a faith that sees more fully, that values different things, that appreciates the distance between God and humanity and still seeks the grace that minds the gap.

In the end, Job is blessed. Job gets all these wonderful, tangible blessings. Yet, he says nothing about them, does he? Job, who had a whole lot to say for twenty chapters, now doesn't say a word. I have a

---

[8] Norman C. Habel, <u>Job: Knox Preaching Guides</u>. (Richmond: John Knox Press, 1981).

feeling that Job doesn't care so much now for all the goats and all the donkeys and all the oxen. I have a feeling Job is not so impressed with all the friends who now start showing up, now that he has money. I have a feeling that while Job loves his ten new children, he still remembers the ten deceased ones. I have a feeling that Job is different, but it isn't because he is shamed or subdued. It is because of what he knows, what he has seen. Job is righteous. He is righteous not because of what he says, what he does or what he owns. Job is righteous because of who he knows, and, I bet, that is all the matters to him now.

I read a story recently of a man passing through his own storm of faith. In it, though, he compared his recovery with that of a parent calling a child home to dinner. "Most of the children in my neighborhood were called home for supper by their mothers. They opened the back doors, wiped their hands on their aprons and yelled, "Willie!" or "Joe!" Either that or they used a bell, bolted to the door frame and loud enough to start the dogs barking in backyards all along the street. But I   was always called home by my father, and he didn't do it in the customary way. He walked down the alley all the way to the lake. If I was close, I could hear his shoes on the gravel before he came into sight. If I was far, I would see him across the surface of the water, emerging out of shadows and into the gray light. He would stand with his hands in the pockets of his windbreaker while he looked for me. This is how he got me to come home. He always came to the place where I was before he called my name."[9]

That is what happens to Job. God goes to where Job is to call him home, to bring him back, to bring him back from precipice of despair and ruin. And, no doubt, Job is different and probably wounded. Anyone going through a storm will be. Yet the only hope for any of us in storm is that of rescue and recovery. Our hope in the storm, in the whirlwind, in the shooting, in the turmoil is the God we know in Christ Jesus. Blessing is not the reacquisition of stuff. Blessing is the one who saves and recovers. It is never about the stuff. It is about the God who shows up. In the mediator of Jesus, justice, wisdom and mercy are all offered through a suffering more profound than that of even Job. In Christ, we have a friend, an advocate and a redeemer. And that is the

---

[9] Dennis Covington, Salvation on Sand Mountain. (New York: Addison-Wesley, 1995).

difference - before, during and after the storm. Anything else, is just a plus.

Thanks be to God.

Every Day I Write the Book
Revelation 1: 4-8

John to the seven churches that are in Asia: Grace to you and peace from him who is and who was and who is to come, and from the seven spirits who are before his throne, ⁵ and from Jesus Christ, the faithful witness, the firstborn of the dead, and the ruler of the kings of the earth. To him who loves us and freed us from our sins by his blood, ⁶ and made us to be a kingdom, priests serving his God and Father, to him be glory and dominion forever and ever. Amen.

⁷ Look! He is coming with the clouds; every eye will see him, even those who pierced him; and on his account all the tribes of the earth will wail. So it is to be. Amen. ⁸ "I am the Alpha and the Omega," says the Lord God, who is and who was and who is to come, the Almighty.

Julie reads all the time. She reads quickly. She reads critically. She reads while doing other things. She can multi-task. She can read a book, watch a TV show, talk on the phone, and tell me something to do all at the same time. It is pretty remarkable. I, on the other hand, like books with pictures. Actually, I'm not that bad. Certainly, though, there as many types of books as there are people who read them - fiction, non-fiction, biographies. All kinds of books in your library. And all kinds of books in your Bible.

There are about as many types of literature in Scripture as there are people who read them. Some people love the poetry of the Psalms. Some do not. Some people like Paul's thick theological letters. Some people like the ancient prophets. Some people would rather pull teeth than read Deuteronomy. I love it. There are favorites like Matthew, Mark, Luke and John. And then. and then there's Revelation. Special is the person who likes Revelation. You generally don't hear people remark: "I can't wait to go home tonight and curl up with John's Revelation!"

Revelation is just a different animal altogether. With its strange visions, bizarre descriptions and down-right frightening stories, people have generally steered clear of it. This is nothing new. Revelation has never been a favorite. It has always been "odd man out." Like its physical place in the Bible, it has always been on the fringe. It was the last book welcomed for the canon of Scripture by early church leaders. Many early bishops were skeptical of its authenticity. Later church leaders also were cautious. Martin Luther did not think it should have been included in Scripture. John Calvin wrote commentaries on every book of the New Testament except one - Revelation. Revelation is odd man out because it is such an odd book. It is hard to understand. It is difficult to integrate into one's everyday life of faith and discipleship. Revelation attracts odd people. It has been fertile ground for all kinds of people trying to force bizarre and dangerous interpretations. Still, Revelation is Scripture and thus God's word, nonetheless.

Before we hold our breath and jump in, there are a couple things you need to know. First, Revelation isn't really a book, but a letter. Written by John from the island of Patmos, the letter was circulated among seven churches in present day Turkey. It was written in the latter half of the first century, which is important because believers then experienced great hardship. They shared in famines, earthquakes, political suffering, and the fall of Jerusalem's beloved temple to an oppressive Roman government. Christians were beginning to be persecuted. Christians were desirous of some hopeful news. Second, the news it offers is about the "end-times." If God's story with humanity has a beginning and middle, there needs to be an end. When you write a book, it needs all three. Revelation is the attempt to look into some future and do that. Third, Revelation was written in a style of literature. It is a style of literature called apocalyptic literature. Revelation, along with a few other books, were written in this odd, cryptic style. Because to try to speak of a time and place one cannot see and cannot know, one has to speak differently. Fourth, good people of strong faith will interpret Revelation differently. Some hear John speaking plainly – telling how things will literally happen. Some hear John speaking symbolically – revealing how the oppressor Rome will meet its end. Some hear John speaking metaphorically – providing windows into spiritual truths. All are certainly fair, and I will be guided by each of those as I seek to preach in the coming weeks. With those things in mind, we approach Revelation... if rather carefully and hesitantly. Today's scripture comes from the first chapter. [text]
Imagine if you will, that you are stuck out on Alcatraz, that island prison in the middle of San Francisco Bay - isolated, hopeless, removed

from the world. This is John. He has been exiled to the rocky island of Patmos, not unlike the birdman of Alcatraz. He is imprisoned. Yet the imprisonment is probably the easiest struggle of recent struggles. He has suffered terribly from persecutions during this time. Now he is out on this island, with time for himself, time with his heart and his mind. He sits there, and with eyes closed, heart wide open and a mind of faith, he sees. And this is what he sees:

> *"Look, he comes. He is coming in the clouds and everyone will see him, everyone even who pierced him, and all the tribes of the earth …and they will all cry."*

This is what John sees. Now, you better get ready because there will be a lot more of that. John's Revelation is an entire recording of what he sees. "And I saw, and I saw, and I saw." So you will hear that phrase again and again. John is doing what just about any of us would do in that situation. He closes his eyes, opens his heart and with the mind of faith, he looks. He does this throughout Revelation. This is his vision. Now, in attempting to do the same, some people have quite differing visions, different visions of the completion of God's story. Some see the world drying up and blowing away. Some see it withering away in silence. Some see armies arriving or bombs dropping. Some see Christ coming. Some seem him coming back happy. Some see him coming back angry. Some see him showing up a bit tardy. Revelation is what John sees.

John isn't the first one to see such things, by the way. Zechariah did too. Way back in the Old Testament, Zechariah closed his eyes, opened his heart and with a mind of faith he saw too. He was bearing the burden of a broken land, of a disappointing world of sin and violence. He saw God coming and speaking.

"I will pour out on the house of David and the inhabitants of Jerusalem a spirit of compassion and supplication so that when they look on him whom they have pierced, they shall mourn for him, as one mourns for an only child and weeps bitterly over him, as one weeps over a first–born. The land itself shall mourn."

Zechariah saw people mourning for a messiah they wounded, as if they realized their loss and felt their guilt. John sees something very similar, doesn't he? And yet, John's vision is unique.

First of all, it is Christ who is coming. Now, this is important. When it was announced that someone was "coming," that was usually cause for fear and dread. People were familiar with having some foreign warrior or Roman general marching in and causing great harm. It was nice to have someone *else* coming for a change. It was nice to have *Christ* coming in particular. It was a pleasant change to have one coming that was *for* them, someone on *their* side for once, coming to *their* aid. The arrival of a new king was usually bad news. Christ is good news. Christ coming is always, forever good news.

Secondly, everyone gets a view. Note the language of the scripture. Christ is not withheld from anyone. No one *can't* see him because of hard heart. No one can't see him because of a bad attitude, sorted religious history. No one *can't* see him because of they live here or they live there, because they are this type or person or that type, because they go to that church and not this one. Everyone gets to see him. Every tribe of every nation.

Moreover, even those who wounded him are allowed to see him. For John, this would likely mean the Romans, the ones who "who pierced his side." We can include, though, anyone who is prone to wound him, willfully, carelessly or indifferently. We could include those who pierce his side, but also those who stab him in the back, who kick him when he is down, who twist his arm or cut thorns in his side. We could include those who break his heart. We could include his enemies, his persecutors, his tormentors, his sympathizers who turned against him, his friends who turned their back on him. All who pierced him, they all see him. They all get a good view. They all experience, see, feel and know. And they all will cry. They cry. Why do they cry? Who knows? Why does anyone cry? Some weep in loss and grief. Some weep in surprise. Some weep with change. Learning from Zechariah, it seems that they weep out of guilt. In any case, this is emotional.

I mentioned earlier about Julie and her books - how she reads a lot and how she reads rather critically. Julie likes many books but is uninspired by others. It takes something special for her to truly love a book. Oddly, the book has to be awful for her to love it! It's the truth. After reading the last page, if Julie is able to close the book and begin sobbing, then it is a good book. If she says, "that was the most awful thing in the world," then she absolutely loves it. Certainly, this confused me for years. I realize now that a really good book is one which is tragic and beautiful, one which is lovely and deep. That is the way it is. The best, most complete, most powerful stories are the ones that cut us to the core and speak to our inner longings.

Such, of course, is the case with the story of this world. Tragic. Beautiful. Lovely. Deep. In the end, that is our story. In the end, Christ comes ... and that is good. And everyone is part of it ... and that is good. And everyone weeps ... and that is good too. When you read Revelation, when you come to the end of this book, you must remember this. "This is good news." Too many people try to make it bad news, but it is good news. That is the point. When we come to the end of this world as we know it, when the story of this world is completed, it will be good. And it will be good because of the One who writes it. Every day he writes the book. He is the alpha and the omega. The writes the beginning, middle and end. The story of this world will wrap itself around the story of Christ. He is the Word. He is the Holy Alphabet. By Christ, the story of this world is told. By Christ, our own stories are told.

If we wrote the book, the story would be quite different. If every day we wrote the book... Chapter one – we didn't really get involved. Chapter two - we think we fell in love with him. We said we'd stand by him in the middle of chapter three. But we were up to our old tricks in chapters four, five and six.[10] No, we can't write such good books well. But thanks goodness, we don't write the book. Christ writes the book. Every day. From its beginning to its beautiful ending. It is the Word of God, even the Word of God when it comes to us in old scary Revelation. And it is good news. Because the Word is full of grace and truth.

Thanks be to God.

---

[10] Adapted from "Every day I Write the Book," Elvis Costello, <u>Punch the Clock</u>. (London: F-Beat Records, 1983).

Crescendo
Revelation 5: 1-14

Then I saw in the right hand of the one seated on the throne a scroll written on the inside and on the back, sealed with seven seals; ²and I saw a mighty angel proclaiming with a loud voice, "Who is worthy to open the scroll and break its seals?" ³And no one in heaven or on earth or under the earth was able to open the scroll or to look into it. ⁴And I began to weep bitterly because no one was found worthy to open the scroll or to look into it. ⁵Then one of the elders said to me, "Do not weep. See, the Lion of the tribe of Judah, the Root of David, has conquered, so that he can open the scroll and its seven seals." ⁶Then I saw between the throne and the four living creatures and among the elders a Lamb standing as if it had been slaughtered, having seven horns and seven eyes, which are the seven spirits of God sent out into all the earth. ⁷He went and took the scroll from the right hand of the one who was seated on the throne. ⁸When he had taken the scroll, the four living creatures and the twenty-four elders fell before the Lamb, each holding a harp and golden bowls full of incense, which are the prayers of the saints. ⁹They sing a new song: "You are worthy to take the scroll and to open its seals, for you were slaughtered and by your blood you ransomed for God saints from every tribe and language and people and nation; ¹⁰you have made them to be a kingdom and priests serving our God, and they will reign on earth." ¹¹Then I looked, and I heard the voice of many angels surrounding the throne and the living creatures and the elders; they numbered myriads of myriads and thousands of thousands, ¹²singing with full voice, Worthy is the Lamb that was slaughtered to receive power and wealth and wisdom and might and honor and glory and blessing!" ¹³Then I heard every creature in heaven and on earth and under the earth and in the sea, and all that is in them, singing, "To the one seated on the throne and to the Lamb be blessing and honor and glory and might forever and ever!" ¹⁴And the four living creatures said, "Amen!" And the elders fell down and worshiped.

In 1967 the Beatles released one of the most important popular rock-n-roll albums of history, Sgt. Pepper's Lonely-Hearts Club Band.[11] The recording was filled with a variety of musical sounds and styles, with unique instrumentations and inventive studio technology. Of the

---

[11] John Lennon and Paul McCartney. "A Day in the Life." Sgt. Pepper's Lonely-Hearts Club Band. (London: Parlophone Records, 1967).

many remarkable things about the album, though, was the last song, "A Day in the Life." The song begins with a soft note and the quiet, melancholy voice of John Lennon. It begins to build, from a simple piano, to the sound of drums, then guitars, then horns, and eventually a full orchestra. You hear a countdown, like a rocket launch. (10, 9, 8, ...) The sound gathers quickly and begins to grow in volume, intensity and ferocity, like a thunderstorm gathering on a hot August southern night. You know the thunderclap is coming, one certain to be louder and closer than what you have ever heard before. You want to take cover, but there isn't time. "Look out. Here it comes!" But then…. something different. Something you didn't expect. No clap of thunder. No explosion of noise. Instead, a little piano note. Dink. Dink. Dink. Is that it? What happened? The song continues. And there will be another crescendo at the end, but from this point forward, everything is different.

I'm sure this sounds like a stretch, but this is not unlike what we find here in the fifth chapter of Revelation. In the middle of the last song of God's grand recording, there is a gathering storm. The unique style and inventive language employed by John takes on a frenzied, alarming quality. Something is happening and happening quickly! John's crescendo actually begins back in chapter four. This is, by most accounts, the center piece and essential window into John's Revelation. There in chapter four John lays out an amazing vision of something he has seen. He now sees in heaven, a door open and a throne. There is more. There are ornaments and accessories. There is lightening. There is thunder. There are four six-winged creatures with innumerable eyes and unceasing voices. And there is singing - lots of singing. Singing, day and night, louder, brighter and stronger. Soon all living creatures join in the chorus. They sing an old song. One familiar to those who have read Isaiah: "Holy, holy, holy the Lord God Almighty, the whole earth is full of his glory, he one who was and is and who is to come."

But this is not all. They seem to be wanting something, needing something, anticipating something. Perhaps it is the scroll that rests in the hands of the one on the throne. What is in the scroll? We don't know. It is sealed, sealed very tightly. We understand that it has something to do with "what takes place next." It has something to do with a conclusion, an ending. It has to do with the culmination of

God's story with humanity. So we don't know, but there seems to be quite a bit of clamoring to find out about it. All these gathering, singing, creatures want to know. They have waited a long time. They have waited through the heart ache and suffering. They have waited through the sin, hate and mess of the world. They have waited long enough. They have waited, no doubt, till the end of God's grand song. And they want to know now. "How does this end? I suppose they come with their own wonder and their own questions. They come with their anger and their hurts, their anxiousness and their doubts. They want to know, "What is there, in the scroll?"

I mentioned last week how Revelation is such an odd book, how it generally makes folks uncomfortable, how it is difficult to read, to hear, certainly to preach. It offers strange images, frightening visions and discomforting prospects. It has a hard reputation for the bizarre and has kept folks at a distance. I mentioned last week how good Christians might interpret the same book differently. Some hear John speaking plainly – telling how things will literally happen. Some hear John speaking symbolically – revealing how the oppressor Rome will meet its end. Some hear John speaking metaphorically – providing windows into spiritual truths. And so for these and other reasons, we tend to read at a distance. Ultimately, though, to appreciate Revelation, you just got to jump right in! Doubt, skepticism, piety, whatever. Whatever you think about the book - it doesn't matter. For this to work, you have to dive in. You have to join the large mass of people that apparently is gathering here in chapter four and, with some faithful imagination, be part of the story! Because, if you are honest, their questions are also our questions! We wouldn't mind a peak at this "story of the world" scroll either.

There is a crowd. The crowd seems to be a gathering from across generations of believers. There is a crescendo of noise. The orchestral is finding its note, like before a grand performance. The crowd is buzzing, like in Greensboro on a tournament Sunday in March. The gallery is marching, like on the 16th hole at Augusta in April. They've waited long enough. They can barely contain themselves. They want an answer. They want a result. And to appreciate Revelation you have to join them. You have to be part of all these who are gathering, who span the generations, to be part of this "great reveal."

But alas... the scroll won't open! It is sealed tightly. It seems not just anyone can pry the story out. So, the singing stops. The people start wondering, "who is worthy enough to open this scroll?" That is what they ask. "Who is worthy enough to open this scroll and allow us to see the story of God in its fulfillment." So now, all these thousands upon thousands of believers are now apparently just standing there, looking at this little scroll, shut up so very tightly that not one of the thousands upon thousands can get open. And John begins to cry.

One of the elders speaks: "Wait! I know who will open it! I remember now. A lion! A great and terrible lion. He will open it. We have always known he would." This idea is actually an old one. Since the earliest days, that is who they have pinned their hopes on: a David-like warrior messiah, one who would come and fight God's battles and wreak vengeance on enemies. The prototype was the lion, the king of the juggle. The fierce and powerful beast with the force to rip the arms and legs off enemies and a voice to bellow a sound that would shut out every other voice. This is the great Lion of God. "Yes, a lion will open the scroll!" No doubt, the culmination of the crescendo will be the lion!

But then…. Something happens. Something different. Something you didn't expect. There is no explosive roar. Instead something else. Like the singular piano note instead of an explosion of sound… Dink. Dink. Dink. A lamb. Not a lion. A lamb. A lamb shows up. And not even a very strong one either. A slaughtered lamb. "Him? That is it? He is the one who can get that scroll open?" A lamb? Can you imagine a bigger about-face? Lions are fierce and strong, loud and proud. Lambs are none of that. Lions roar. Lambs bleat. Lions rule. Lambs roam. In fact, lions eat lambs! Any other beast at least has a fighting chance in this world. An elephant is big. A porcupine has needles. Sting rays have those sharp fins. Even the tiniest ant has a bite to make your finger swell. The lamb has none of that. The lamb doesn't even have a good defense. Some frogs have poisonous skin. Some lizards blend in with the trees. Birds can fly away. Moles can tunnel down. Lambs have none of that. It is no wonder they became good targets for sacrifice in days of old. How hard would it be to sacrifice a lamb? A lamb in this world, no matter how perfect, how divine, is doomed. Gosh, we just can't help ourselves but slaughter it. There he is. In the strangest crescendo in history, when the world waited for a lion, the world gets a lamb.

The answer to every question, the hope to every despair, the period to every sentence and the conclusion to every drama is not a lion for your vengeance, but a lamb for your deliverance. You would think someone might protest, "Hey, we ordered the lion." But no. In fact, it seems they LIKE the lamb! It is, apparently, better than they had imagined. A cheer goes up. The singing begins again. In fact, it is a NEW song.

> *"...for the lamb ransomed for God*
> *saints from every tribe and language and people and nation."*

They know now that the only answer that would work is the lamb. For the lamb on the throne is the only thing this slaughtering world could not defeat. For Christ on the throne is only way that a despairing world can be saved. And John, who spends so much of his time telling us when he sees, now tells us what he HEARS:

> *"the voice of angels and living creatures, numbering in the myriads of myriads and thousands of thousands, singing in full voice: 'worthy is the lamb! The lamb slaughtered. To receive power and wealth and wisdom and might and honor and glory and blessing ..."* (And probably a few more adjectives if he had breath).

They sing. And they never stop singing.

At the end of the greatest album in history, the crescendo remerges on the Beatle's last song. Just like before, it comes, with piano and drum and guitar and orchestra with flute and harp and horn and bass and string and pipe and timpani. And it builds and builds like before, but this time the ending comes. Powerful, uniform, stunning and expansive. Multiple hands on multiple pianos and the full volume of the full orchestra hitting one note perfectly. Yet the beauty of the greatest album in history is that the last note doesn't really end ... it just goes on.

For those who remember, those old albums had little threads at the end of a record that would throw your needle back so it wouldn't fall off into oblivion. Usually, it was just static you heard. But in this, the greatest album in history, there isn't silence. There is sound. The last note on the album falls on that little thread at the end of the album, so the song actually never ends. The note just keeps playing forever and ever and ever. It is awesome, like the lamb, in the crescendo in God's great and glorious final word.

Thanks be to God.

Wash. Rinse. Repeat.
Revelation 7: 9-17

After this I looked, and there was a great multitude that no one could count, from every nation, from all tribes and peoples and languages, standing before the throne and before the Lamb, robed in white, with palm branches in their hands. **10** *They cried out in a loud voice, saying, "Salvation belongs to our God who is seated on the throne, and to the Lamb!"* **11** *And all the angels stood around the throne and around the elders and the four living creatures, and they fell on their faces before the throne and worshiped God,* **12** *singing, "Amen! Blessing and glory and wisdom and thanksgiving and honor and power and might be to our God forever and ever! Amen."* **13** *Then one of the elders addressed me, saying, "Who are these, robed in white, and where have they come from?"* **14** *I said to him, "Sir, you are the one that knows." Then he said to me, "These are they who have come out of the great ordeal; they have washed their robes and made them white in the blood of the Lamb.* **15** *For this reason they are before the throne of God, and worship him day and night within his temple, and the one who is seated on the throne will shelter them.* **16** *They will hunger no more, and thirst no more; the sun will not strike them, nor any scorching heat;* **17** *for the Lamb at the center of the throne will be their shepherd, and he will guide them to springs of the water of life, and God will wipe away every tear from their eyes."*

Have you ever been at a party and not known a sole? You attend the event and you go alone, but you know no one. For what seems like forever, you shuffle about, stirring a drink, looking at furniture, attempting to speak to people who all already know each other. It is terribly uncomfortable. But then, *finally*, you recognize someone walking through the door! Hurray! Someone familiar, someone to talk to! This, I have wondered, is what John must be experiencing here. After six chapters of amazing visions and strange sounds, after verses of the bizarre, multi-headed beasts and many-horned creatures, John finally sees something familiar.

Let me remind you that Revelation is essentially a reporting of this very unusual vision that John has while stuck out on this island in the Mediterranean. Persecuted and prosecuted, John is in prison. In the stillness of his time he has, John looks out with an open heart and sees the future that is the completion of God's work. Now because it is seeing what cannot be seen and describing what cannot be described, the language is unusual. Most of what he sees is unsettling. It is strange and bizarre. So when some actual *people* showed up to this grand party, you can understand if he might be a bit relived. There in the seventh chapter comes a great multitude of people, swarms of people from every land and of every tongue, wearing robes and carrying branches. After all four frightening horsemen, after creatures with six wings and faces full of eyes, and after falling stars and quaking earth, finally some people! Moreover, these are not just any people, but a *redeemed* people - a great many of them, too many too count in fact.

It is interesting, by the way, that Revelation remains a bit mysterious here. Revelation generally does not shy away from being specific. Revelation never hesitates to count things. Just moments earlier Revelation counted out the number of those in the tribes of Israel (144,000). Yet here, Revelation is suddenly vague. This one is too much to count, too overwhelming to specify. Suffice to say, this is a great multitude, from all over, more than one can count, more than one could imagine.

Yet there is one who suddenly steps forward and speaks to John. There is one angelic figure who has questions for John. "Who are these people?" he asks John, "and where do they come from?" Before John can answer, the man answers his own question. "These are the they who have come out of the great tribulation. They have washed their robes and made them white in the blood of the lamb." Maybe John didn't answer because he would have gotten the answer wrong. He likely wouldn't have answered *that* way! The angelic figure offers an unusual answer to his own question. To the question of "who they are" - no names are given. To the question of "where they are from" - no location is told. Where are they all from? They are from a place called tribulation. That is where they all are from. Tribulation.

Now, we all know that one of the dangers of Revelation is that a few side-lined believers like to take the side-lined Scripture and draw out of it rather out-of-bounds conclusions. They love to literalize one verse or one vision. They would love to compute and calculate a time or place of this or that. "Now is the time of tribulation," they would declare! "Now is the time of Christ's coming," they would pinpoint. A fellow named William Miller did so. In the mid 1800's, William Miller knew just enough to be dangerous. He convinced enough people to see his vision and they formed their own group. Millerist! Miller knew the mind of God! He knew so, so much that he even started setting dates for God. He did the math. He did the analytics. "Christ would come in 1843." So, all his people gathered in their white robes and waited. Of course, that didn't happen. So, William did some revisions. More math, more analytics. "1847 it shall be." Then 1847 came and went, and William's followers revised poor William!

It is never smart to start calculating God. Nonetheless, William and ilk are not all bad. What William and his ilk do right is that they are unafraid to jump in Revelation and, with faithful imagination, let it speak to them and their time. It is really the best way to read Revelation. Not to check your brain at the introduction, but to jump-in and, with an unafraid spirit, share in the story. In doing so, we often find, among the bizarre, a few familiar faces and abiding truths.

The scripture says that all these people came out of a place called Great Tribulation. It is certainly valuable to try to figure when and what exactly that Great Tribulation was all about. Another option is to do what John did and just listen. Stuck on the island that is called Patmos, John knew about tribulation, and John knew all about the tribulation of the early church. John did not have to ask if his tribulation was the same tribulation of his vision. He didn't need to. He just shared in the story. And that is what faithful Christians have done for years with Scripture. They hear their story in THE Story. For they too knew about tribulation. They too were either from that place or trying to get out of it. All kinds of Christians, every single Christian church since the dawn of Acts has lived in tribulation. So John didn't have to get into specifics. Everybody knew about the place called Tribulation.

See, Revelation isn't so odd. You get into it and look at it a certain way, it isn't so odd. You see familiar things. Everybody recognizes tribulation. Everyone recognizes laundry. Yes, that is what I said. Laundry. That is the next thing you see in this story. Laundry. All these people make it out of tribulation and into the grace of the throne of God … only to do laundry. Revelation 7.14. "*These are the ones who have come out of the great tribulation. They have washed their robes and made them white, white with the blood of the lamb."* That is laundry. If you give yourself to these scriptures closely enough, you will find all kinds of familiar things, and here in verse 14 is laundry. Just as everyone is familiar with tribulation, everyone on the planet knows about laundry.

Now, for some of you, this image may be a frightening as anything else already described in this unusual book. The notion that when we finally make it through our respective tribulations and finally reach the throne of God there is waiting for us a pile of laundry, well, that could be alarming. I see the panic in your eyes. We don't know much about the redeemed, just that they all go through tribulation and none come out unblemished by it. We don't know much about them, just that all hail from tribulation and once they get through it, they all have laundry to do.

We had to buy a new washer recently. Not a very exciting purchase, but a necessary one. You have to have clean clothes. Therefore you buy a new washer. This is nice, except you have to install it, and new washers, like everything else, come with instructions. There is a large book of instructions, telling you not only about how to install your washer, but how to wash with it. The book offers four pages dedicated to telling you HOW to wash clothes. There is the sorting section. Separate white, light and colorfast items from dark and non-colorfast items. Separate heavily soiled from lightly soiled items. Separate lacy or delicate items from more heavy items. There is the preparing section. Empty pockets. Brush off lint and loose dirt. Remove decorative buttons and buckles. Mends rips to prevent further damage. There is a loading section. Load large items first. Clear items away from the sensor. There is a whole section just on stains! Mildew? Wash with bleach. Soak in oxygen bleach and hot water. Tomato? Pre-treat with stain remover. Baby formula? Pre-treat. Soak for 20 minutes. Oily stains? Treat with prewash remover. Increase water tempt. Rewash. Yellow build-up? Soak in detergent boost of enzymes. Wash in hot water. Add bleach. Wrinkling? Reduce load size. Rinse in cold water. The list goes on. If you need more, you can contact the Soap and Detergent Association. True. The Soap and Detergent Association. I suppose it is a volunteer group, but I can't imagine how.

All these instructions on how to wash, but nowhere in there is there any help in washing the dirt of this world. How do you get out the stain of years of wear and tear? How do you wash out the memories of 9/11? How do you wash out Columbine or Sandy Hook? How do you rub out the sin that imbeds itself in every fiber? That stuff just will not come out. You can't scrub it out. You can't rinse and repeat it out. You can't shout it out. It is the build-up of years of tribulation. And no one, not even the Detergent and Soup Association, has an answer for it. It simply sticks to you like some kind of super dirt.

Those stubborn stains wear on your good will. Even the most laundry-hating of the redeemed might look forward washing all that away. They might actually appreciate washing, rinsing, repeating until it is all gone, gone with the hunger and heartache. Here in the scripture, those who arrived from tribulation don't seem at all bothered by the laundry duty. There seems to be no complaints here. They seem to be more than ok with this schedule, as if they have been waiting to finally wash their robes, to get them white. Having survived the tribulation, peeling off the dirty layers and restoring the soiled rob is a good thing.

Revelation is an odd book. I don't understand the strange metaphors and words. I don't understand how one washes garments in blood to get them white. For that matter, I don't understand how the Lamb in verse 17, suddenly becomes the Shepherd. Strange. But such is the reversal of fortunes and ways in the Kingdom of God, where the first are last and the last first. It is all hard to calculate. But I am not going to try to calculate it. I'm just going to read it and see if it speaks to me. Because I figure, what have we got to lose? What we are washing with here isn't working. We keep washing and rinsing and all we get is more school shootings and more war and more broken homes and more mess and more crushed spirits. What have we got to lose?   With faithful imagination and with hearts wide open, we count ourselves among the redeemed, we join the tribulation-weary souls who gather at that great laundry mat in the sky, where we, along with the rest, wash out the miseries of every Bosnia, Baghdad and Blacksburg, where we rinse out the disappointments and disasters of hidden hearts and in the world's highest places, and where we, like John, might confess, that:

"Never again will we thirst,
never again will we hunger.

The sun will not beat upon us
nor any scorching heat break us.
For the Lamb at the center of the throne is our shepherd
and he will lead us to springs of living waters.

And God will wipe away every tear from every eye."

Thanks be to God.

The Dwelling
Revelation 21:1-6

Then I saw a new heaven and a new earth; for the first heaven and the first earth had passed away, and the sea was no more. ²And I saw the holy city, the new Jerusalem, coming down out of heaven from God, prepared as a bride adorned for her husband. ³And I heard a loud voice from the throne saying, "See, the home of God is among mortals. He will dwell with them; they will be his peoples, and God himself will be with them; ⁴ he will wipe every tear from their eyes. Death will be no more; mourning and crying and pain will be no more, for the first things have passed away."

⁵And the one who was seated on the throne said, "See, I am making all things new." Also he said, "Write this, for these words are trustworthy and true." ⁶Then he said to me, "It is done! I am the Alpha and the Omega, the beginning and the end. To the thirsty I will give water as a gift from the spring of the water of life.

You may not have read much of Revelation, but chances are good you have read this one. Revelation 21. It is a familiar refrain at funerals. It is among the more palatable of John's visions. It lacks strange beasts and unsightly sights found elsewhere in this book. It is a peaceful passage. It describes the calm after the storm, the rest after a wearying battle. Therefore it comes as a sigh of relief, as a deep appreciation for God's victory. It is the culmination of twenty chapters. It is the final word, the last scene. And it is, I would argue, the summation of God's whole word.

This of course doesn't mean it is suddenly easy to interpret. It is still Revelation after all. So we are compelled to read with a different set of ears and see with a different set of eyes. One has to read differently. The message here is opaque. The language is overwhelming. The symbols are many. The images are fluid, the metaphors mixed. Get over it. That is just Revelation, start to finish. Even here in Chapter 21. So, as Revelation draws to a close, one has to imagine the smoke clearing after a battle or imagine the sun rising after a storm. For a great upheaval has happened between good and evil, and John is seeing the other side it. As before, he tells us what he sees. Now, though, what he sees is very different, very different indeed.

John sees "a new heaven and new earth," which is a way to say that the whole of creation is now transformed. The broken world we live in is now different, the tears that were shed in heaven have dried up too. This world is redeemed. John observes that "the sea was no more," which is to say that the chaos of our world has now ceased. Often in Scripture "sea" is a symbol for danger and disorder. Sea is a sign of turmoil. Here, in this vision, after the culmination of God's final work, all that is now gone. Finally, John sees a "New Jerusalem," which is a way of saying that the centerpiece of their religious life has been restored. For Jerusalem was their home - culturally, religiously, socially. And the old Jerusalem had been beaten up and knock down so many times it just limped along, and no one could agree on how to rebuild it anyway. Now, a new Jerusalem, a transformed Jerusalem, this perfect home has been restored, a new relationship has begun, like a marriage between a bride and a groom. It is the union of God's creatures in harmony.

This is what John sees. John, though, also hears, and what he hears is as awesome as what he has seen. A voice, from the throne.

> *³ And I heard a loud voice from the throne saying, "See, the home of God is among mortals. He will dwell with them; they will be his peoples, and God himself will be with them; ⁴ he will wipe every tear from their eyes.*

> *Death will be no more; mourning and crying and pain will be no more, for the first things have passed away."*

A voice speaks. This voice speaks a pronouncement, a blessing. It speaks to the grief of the world. It speaks to the pain of the world. It speaks to the anger of the world. It is powerful. It is beautiful. It is comforting. It is no wonder we like it at funerals. After what people often go through before or during death, they often need to hear about a plan for a world where there is no more mourning, no more crying, no more pain, and no more tears. These are old, old words. Yet this ancient speech still speaks to us today, even in the most painful and contemporary of tragedies. These words are powerful, beautiful and comforting. But these words are also more than even that. These words are important. The importance finds its center in verse three. If there a pinnacle in this final book of the Bible, verse three is that place. It is, in my mind, the summation of the whole of God's story.

"See, the home of God is among mortals."

Now, in my mind, to understand this scripture one has to know what it is like to live out of boxes. I am guessing that most of you have moved at some point. And if you have moved, then you know what it is like to live out of boxes. I moved to Raleigh from Atlanta years ago. I had few possessions, but enough that I couldn't leave them in my car. I lived in someone's attic apartment for six months. All my boxes were at a U-Haul facility on Capital Boulevard in Raleigh. Despite my fastidious planning, I could never get what I needed. "Where is that book? "Where is my winter coat?" "Where are my black shoes? "Where is my phone directory?" I was forever going back and forth to that storage unit. When you live out of boxes you are not living. You are not settled. You are unsettled. You are not at ease. You are restless. You are not at home. You are homeless. And as odd as it sounds, God has been living out of boxes for the entirety of Scripture.

It is true. Since the days of the Exodus, when God traveled with Israel through the wilderness as fire and cloudy pillar, God has been restless. You might remember back in II Samuel, King David took pity on God and tried to build God a home. Noting that he himself had a house of cedar, David felt bad that there was no special dwelling for God. So David decided to build a home for God! God, though, would have none of it.

"Why would you build me a house to dwell in? I have not dwelt in a house since the day that I brought up the people of Israel from Egypt to this day. Instead, I have been moving about in a tent. In all places where I have moved with the people of Israel, did I ever speak a word to any of you saying, 'why have you not built me a house of cedar?'" God doesn't want a house. God wouldn't fit in a house. It made no sense.

And it goes on like that for chapter upon chapter. When Israel is exiled to Babylon, God goes with them. When an itinerant preacher named Jesus comes and travels the countryside, God travels with him. God is forever on the road. There is a transient-ness to God. It is as if God has been living out of boxes or living out of his car, as a transiently homeless person.

You know there is a whole segment of people who live out of their cars.[12] I've learned that this is not a steady percentage of the homeless population. Instead the number fluctuates, depending on the economy. These are "mobile homeless," and there have been studies on them. They are not homeless long. They often have some kind of job, but not enough income to secure a permanent residence. The car is often all they have left. Studies indicate that they are rather resilient. They are very careful where they park. They are very quiet about their situation. They are actually adept at making do, staying on top of car insurance and inspections, joining a gym to have access to showers, parking in well-lit, safe, but quiet areas. And moving along to where the job is or, in some cases, moving along to follow a relationship. What they find is that these "mobile homeless" not only come out of homelessness quicker, but they see their plight differently. They see it as short term. They anticipate a time when they once again will park their car in their own driveway.

That is good, because studies also show that before anything can really change for the homeless, they need an address, they need a place to call home. Once they have a place, things can change - jobs, paycheck, Social Security, etc. Until they have a place, though, nothing can fall in place. In Revelation 21, that change happens for God.

"See, the home of God is among mortals."

Now, there are a couple ways to read this scripture. One can read the "see" as in "look," as if John is showing us something new ("Look! Now the dwelling of God is among mortals!"). I think, though, the better reading is "see" as in "do you understand?" ("Do you

---

[12] Ian Urbina, "Keeping it Secret as the Family Car Becomes a Home." New York Times, April 2, 2006. https://www.nytimes.com/2006/04/02/us/02cars.html

understand now? The dwelling of God is among mortals! That is how God dwells. That is where God dwells. That is where God has always dwelled. That is what God has always wanted. Do you understand? The dwelling place of God is among people!").

In any case, this is in many ways a summation of God's work in Scripture. It is a message God has been trying to communicate since the days of Eden. It is a message God showed Israel when the Lord followed them through the wilderness and when God refused David's house. It is a message God lived out with the incarnation. Yes, God wants a home, but God doesn't want a house! God wants a home with the people of God's creation. More than anything else, God wants to be with us. In relationship! *With* us. That is the message.

It is message we keep missing. King David clearly missed it. God had to set him right. But even before that God was sending the message. Jacob also missed the message. One of my favorite stories in the Old Testament is in Genesis. Jacob's dream at Bethel or Jacob's ladder. Jacob has been on the run... homeless, you might say. He falls to sleep one night and dreams of a ladder, reaching to heaven. There God speaks to him. Four times God assures Jacob of God's holy presence. "I am with you. I will keep you. I will bring you. I will not leave you." But when Jacob wakes up, it is as if he didn't hear a word. "Surely the Lord is with this place! How awesome is this place! This place is the house of God and the gate of heaven!" No! No, Jacob. That is not right! God never said that. The Lord is not "with this place." The Lord is with YOU. There is a big difference. That is the promise. Not that God is here or there, but that God is here (within me) and there (within you). Revelation 21 is the summation of all that. After the storm, after the battle, comes truth, comes clarity. "See, the home of God is with people." That has been the truth all along.

Of course, you know the story of Scripture is not simple the story of a homeless God, transient, living out of boxes. It is also the story of a transient people, of a humanity that seems to be trying to avoid God or, in some cases, seeking to find God but not sure how to do so. And the blessing always comes in those moments when we find each other, when the God who lingers and the people who wander embrace, when God's people realize there is not a specific way to be or act in order to find God. Nor is there a precise place with which to escape, an ideology that must be protected or a defined theology to which one must adhere. The case is always... grace. "Can't you see? The home of God is with mortals."

And in that day, in that future, of God's completed work, that will be known, fully and finally.

> *"God will dwell with them.*
> > *And they shall be God's people*
> > *And God himself will be with them."*
> *And God will, in that day...*
> > *Wipe away every tear from their eyes.*
> > *And death shall be no more.*
> > *Neither shall there be mourning,*
> > *nor crying,*
> > *nor pain,*
> > *anymore,*
> > *for the former things*
> > > *would have passed away."*

Thanks be to God.

Full Circle
Revelation 21:22- 22:5

I saw no temple in the city, for its temple is the Lord God the Almighty and the Lamb. 23 And the city has no need of sun or moon to shine on it, for the glory of God is its light, and its lamp is the Lamb. 24 The nations will walk by its light, and the kings of the earth will bring their glory into it. 25 Its gates will never be shut by day—and there will be no night there. 26 People will bring into it the glory and the honor of the nations. 27 But nothing unclean will enter it, nor anyone who practices abomination or falsehood, but only those who are written in the Lamb's book of life.

Then the angel showed me the river of the water of life, bright as crystal, flowing from the throne of God and of the Lamb 2 through the middle of the street of the city. On either side of the river is the tree of life with its twelve kinds of fruit, producing its fruit each month; and the leaves of the tree are for the healing of the nations. 3 Nothing accursed will be found there anymore. But the throne of God and of the Lamb will be in it, and his servants[a] will worship him; 4 they will see his face, and his name will be on their foreheads. 5 And there will be no more night; they need no light of lamp or sun, for the Lord God will be their light, and they will reign forever and ever.

A rt Buchwald never knew his mother.[13]

"Shortly after I was born, my mother was taken away from me or I was taken away from my mother," he writes. "This was done because she was mentally ill. She suffered from severe chronic depression, which required that she be committed to a private sanitarium. She never recovered and, eventually, when my father ran out of money, she was placed in a state hospital in upper New York for thirty-five years - the rest of her life. I never saw my mother, although she lived until I was in my thirties. When I was a child, they would not let me visit her. When I grew up, I did not want to. I preferred the mother I had invented to the one I would find in the hospital. The denial has been very heavy burden to carry around all these years, and to this day I still

---

[13] Art Buchwald. Leaving Home. (New York: GP Putnam's Sons, 1993).

haven't figured it all out. When I grew up and was in therapy in DC with Dr. RC Morse, discussion about my mother took up quite a bit of our time. As with many children who never knew their mothers, I have been on a lifelong search for someone to replace her. The search has taken more time than my work, although I know that I will never find a surrogate, I can't seem to stop looking.

In 1960, at age sixty-seven, she died. There was a funeral in New York. I didn't make it because I was in Paris at the time. I was shaken by the news. Since the funeral had taken place a week before the letter arrived, it was obviously too late for me to attend, and there was no need to go home. So even when she was buried, I did not see her.

My wife Ann told me that I had walked in our dining room and sat down. She asked what was wrong, and I blurted out, "My mother died," and immediately started to cry. When we grieve, tears and guilt get mixed together. My sisters always tried to console me by saying that, even if I had gone to see my mother, she wouldn't have known who I was. They said that I would have been as much a stranger to her as she was to me. This thought has helped, but sometimes, particularly at night, I think that I was a coward not to go and see her.

In spite of my never having seen her, she was very much a part of me. In days of my darkest depression I would cry for her. When I told my story to Dr. Morse, the next morning, he said he was not surprised by my tears. I had gagged up a whole lifetime of material deprivation."

Buchwald writes all this in a memoir entitled *Leaving Home.* And after reading I wondered how you leave a home you don't remember?" How do you miss what you never experienced? Art Buchwald never knew his mother. Never spoke to her. He can't remember what she looked like, sounded like, smelled like. He never knew her touch, her anger, her humor, her aggravating idiosyncrasies. If he had not seen a picture, she could walk right past him and he would not know it. And yet he wanted her back. How does one long for what one didn't experience? It is not uncommon, you know, for children, even grown children, to long for mothers they never knew. As common as it is for children to long for mothers they did know. Or to long for mothers they had once. Or to long for mothers they wish they had.

I remember Julie's pregnancies like they were yesterday. It was remarkable. She ate for two. She walked for two. She breathed for two. Because she walked, the baby walked. Of course, when she was awake, the slept and when she was trying to sleep, the baby was awake. But other than that, they are two in one. It was remarkable. And short lived. In general, in the span of a lifetime, it is a brief moment. For soon there is separation. There is delivery, then a roll, then a crawl, then a step, then a word, then the car keys. But even as we go, even as we need to go and separate because it is healthy to do so, there is some part of us that desires to go back. To go back to a place where we were safe, to go back to the place where we were cared for, to go back to the place where we were wrapped in arms of love and care that overwhelmed and eased every sense.

Many psychologists say it is a deep, deep desire. One says that "there is a life- long yearning... to return, if not to the womb, then to a state of union or symbiosis. It is a state for which every human being strives. We have no conscious memories of being there or leaving. But once it was ours and we had to let it go. And while the cruel game of giving up what we love in order to grow must be replayed at each new stage of life development, this is our first and perhaps hardest renunciation: The loosing, leaving and letting go of that paradise. And although we do not remember it, we also never forget it."[14]   Apparently, we remember and desire that "time of harmony, wholeness, that time of unbreakable safety, unconditional love. And while we fiercely protect the boundaries of self that clearly demark the "you" from the "me," we also yearn to recapture the "lost paradise of that ultimate connection."

There is something to this - that in each of is a need to return to that which we hardly knew, something of "harmony and wholeness and unbreakable safety and unconditional love." That is the sad story, is it not - the aching in each of us, the hurt in all of us, the sin that consumes every one of us? Consider the child who regresses in his behavior to get attention. Consider the adult who marries for the wrong reason. Consider the family that just keeps buying their way to a perfect world. Consider the patient who never gets enough therapy. Consider the man

---

[14] Judith Viorst. <u>Necessary Losses</u>. (New York: Simon & Schuster, 1986).

who never finds anyone good enough to marry. Consider the woman who never will leave the house of her childhood. Consider the couple who doesn't understand why they fight. Consider the thousands of religions people who make their way to Jerusalem? Yeah. We seek it in religion.

Three religions make their way into the holy city of Jerusalem. The ancient city within a city, with ancient walls to provide a barricaded sacred space against the world. Yet, all these very different people go there. They come to the rock. They come to the western wall. They come to the Church of the Holy Sepulcher. And they have come for years, wanting to touch to be part of the holy. All apparently seeking to return "to a place of harmony and wholeness, that time of unbreakable safety, unconditional love, to recapture the lost paradise of that ultimate connection."

You know Scripture does that. The Bible comes to full circle in many ways. As we come to the end of Revelation, as John sees what he sees in the closing of this world, what John sees, in some ways, is the Bible in reverse. It is a return to the garden.

Curiously, for the first time, John tells us what he doesn't see. He has spent twenty-two chapters telling what he does see. Now he tells us what he does not see, what to him is an obvious omission in this new world. The first thing he does not see is a temple. "I do not see a temple." "Temple," of course, meant worship. Now, for those who struggle with getting up in the morning, this might be good news. "Oh, good, I don't have to go to church in heaven. Thank goodness!" Of course, it is more than just that though. Temple was a central part of the Hebrew story. For the people of God it was the core of their identity. But now, in John's vision, there is no such returning. There is no temple for worship. We do not need it. There is no need for the temple, because the place we go will be worshipful enough.

John continues. In this vision, John sees no sun or moon to offer light. They are not needed. There is enough light by virtue of the light of Christ. And in this place, John sees a big grand street. So there is commerce, people, activity... life! In this place, John sees no gates. No, in this Jerusalem, the gates are open. There is no Muslim district, Christian district, Jewish district. There is no security check point.

There is no green card or border patrol. It is an open border. There is welcome. In this place, there is a river- pure, clear and clean.

Then John sees one last thing. After all this seeing in Revelation, John shares one last thing he sees. There along the backs of this river, John sees a tree, a tree of life, with leaves for the healing of the nations. And with that the reader might begin to recall a different garden, with another river and a similar tree. We begin to hearken back to the last time such a thing was mentioned in Scripture. We hearken way back to Genesis, when the man and woman left the paradise and walked out right past a tree, never to see it again... until now...when in some great providence the story of God comes full circle and by the grace of God we are back in the garden, by the river and under the tree.

They call them family trees. When I was a child, we created one in Sunday School. We cut out trunks, branches and leaves from colored construction paper. My friend Paul did one too. Paul had red paper, so he cut out apples. In his tree, he placed an apple for his mother, an apple for his father, and an apple for him. He had an apple for his sister too, but her apple was on the ground.

The irony is that five years later, when we were 13, his then 17 year-old-sister did drop from the tree. She ran away from home. She just left. I guess, gone to look for something she thought she lost. I was too young to remember the details. I recall it obviously being a devastating moment for father and mother. I then recall, though, several years later she was in an automobile accident in Atlanta. They asked her who they should call. She said, "Call my parents." They showed up. Of course. Because they were in the same tree. She called them because, well, she longed for something.

Healing is what she needed. Healing is what we all need. Healing is what this world needs. And healing is what we will get. When one day we all gather at the river, under the tree of life, that is, as the scripture says, for the healing of the nations. And no doubt, the healing of all the people -brothers sister, fathers and mothers.

Thanks be to God.

Preaching Seasons

Getting Rid of the Stuff
Jeremiah 33:14-18

The days are surely coming, says the LORD, when I will fulfill the promise I made to the house of Israel and the house of Judah. ¹⁵ In those days and at that time I will cause a righteous Branch to spring up for David; and he shall execute justice and righteousness in the land. ¹⁶ In those days Judah will be saved, and Jerusalem will live in safety. And this is the name by which it will be called: "The LORD is our righteousness."

¹⁷ For thus says the LORD: David shall never lack a man to sit on the throne of the house of Israel, ¹⁸ and the Levitical priests shall never lack a man in my presence to offer burnt offerings, to make grain offerings, and to make sacrifices for all time.

If you have come to church enough in the days before Christmas, you might recall that we get a full dose of Old Testament readings from the prophets. The lectionary at Advent is always giving us prophets. This is a problem primarily because prophets are forever bringing harsh news, pointing out all the problems in the world. Prophets are forever calling for repentance, and this is the last thing people want to hear at Christmas time. It is a hard-enough preparing for the magic of Christmas with the world we live in. It is a hard enough manipulating our minds in merriment, gathering all the presents and investing in all the parties with a world that is being blown up all around us. We sure do not need the prophets pointing out what we already know. People do not come to church to feel worse about what we already know about the world!

So, when given a book like Jeremiah, Micah or Zephaniah, the tendency is to look around the verses for something palatable, for some "Jeremiah Light," if you will. Unfortunately, the preacher won't find it, not with Jeremiah anyway. Jeremiah always seems to have something to complain about. Jeremiah is consistently negative. He is negative in the first chapter when God called him to be a prophet. He doesn't like the idea and obeys under protest. It is quality that has served Jeremiah well, though, for there is a lot to complain about.

Jeremiah is an emotional type. He looks around and sees nothing but a mess.

"Oh, the walls of my heart break. I cannot keep silent, for I hear the sound of trumpets. The whole land is laid waste."

Jeremiah is incensed and angry. He sees corruption, greed, cruelty, indifference to God, indifference to neighbors, particularly to neighbors in need.

"They set traps for people. Their houses are full of treachery. They have become rich and great and fat and conniving. Their wickedness knows no bounds. They seek no justice, the cause of the fatherless. They do not defend the rights of the needy."

Jeremiah is insightful, piercing in his judgments.

"My people have committed two evils; they have forsaken the lord, the fountain of living waters, and they have hewed out cisterns for themselves, broken ones that can hold no water."

All this is not very attractive to folks at Christmas. It isn't conducive to holiday cheer. It wasn't attractive then either, by the way. The reaction to Jeremiah was always fierce and brutal. He was shouted out and shouted down. He was arrested, beaten and thrown in jail more than once. He was banned from the city. He found a scribe to write down his words and read them in the temple. They took the script and burned it. Jeremiah and his ilk are tiresome. They have an agenda and will not let it go. Even in the happiest time of the year, when we are trying so very hard to be happy, Jeremiah is relentless. Being a prophet, though, means that Jeremiah also shares a word from God, and these words are the most pointed.

"My eyes are upon all of their ways. They are not hid from me, nor is their iniquity concealed from my eyes. I will doubly recompense their iniquity and their sin, because they have polluted my land with the carcasses of their detestable idols."

This what got my attention this week. This last line: "The carcasses of detestable idols." It is unclear what Jeremiah means by that. Some scholars think he could be referring to real animals, creatures that were set aside for glory, but are now lunch for birds of prey. Most think it refers to fashioned idols that were destroyed by rivals or that simply fell apart. The idols worshippers likely found something better, something new and improved, then simply cast aside the old idols. They were thrown out the car window so to speak, and left to litter the roadside. "They have polluted my land with the carcasses of detestable idols."

I assume by now you have started your Christmas list. I started mine months ago. I assume you have started a list because you have many people on your list. We all do. Maybe you began on Black Friday. You have a lot to buy for your children and your siblings. You have a lot to buy for your parents and grandparents, your uncles, aunts and cousins. Of course, it doesn't end there. You have to buy for your kid's teachers and coaches. You have to buy for your boss and coworkers. You have to buy for your neighbors and friends. You have to buy for bridge partners and supper clubs. You have to buy for your barista, your dentist and your garbage collector. You have a lot of stuff to buy. You can go to Walmart or Target. You can go on-line. You can go to a boutique or the dollar store even, but you will go and buy something. You will buy because you want to. You will buy because you need to, because you are obligated to. Of course, the great thing is that you get stuff too. People will buy *you* stuff. You will get stuff from family members and friends. You will get stuff from the bosses and co-workers, from neighbors, from bridge partners and supper clubs, stuff you definitely need I'm sure. You will enter their houses with a box full of stuff, and you will leave with a box full of stuff. You will buy this stuff and you will receive this stuff because you are celebrating Christmas.

We will spend 600 billion dollars at Christmas. Now, it certainly serves a good economic purpose. It creates income. It creates jobs. Still, do you ever ask yourself, "What am I doing with all this stuff?" I know it is Christmas, but ... really? The biggest trash day of year is December 26th. Did you know that? In December alone, Americans create 25% more waste. One million tons of extra waste discarded. "They have polluted my land with the carcasses of detestable idols."

69

Today's sermon isn't simply about the trash, though that is part of it. Today's sermon isn't simply about the gifts, though that is part of it. Today's sermon is about the purpose. The holiday season lives by this premise: More presents equals better Christmas. More lights equal better Christmas. More activity equals better Christmas. It is the FaceBook fallacy. Of course, we inevitably discover that more stuff just equals more stuff. Ultimately, we can't buy our way into Christmas.

Have you ever known anyone who was *really* into Christmas? Have you known people who were over-the-top with the decor, over-indulged with the food, and over-budget with the investment? Perhaps a part of you feels guilty, like there is something wrong with you for not being like that. Then, perhaps there is another part of you that thinks, "Oh no. There is something wrong with that!" Welcome to Christmas in America. "They have polluted my land with the carcasses of detestable idols." I'm not trying to be a scrooge, but I find it interesting that in recent years holiday consumption seems to rise in direct correlation to a rise in violence. Maybe it is just a coincidence. Maybe I'm speaking out of line, because certainly the world has always been violent. But still, it is curious that things keep blowing up, and we keep buying more stuff.

Idols, you might remember, always seem to be a problem with the people of faith. You might recall that God had no sooner given the ten commandments when God's people promptly went out caste themselves an idol. What happened? How did they manage to violate the second commandment so fast? Listen to the story in Exodus:

When the people saw that Moses was so long in coming down from the mountain, they gathered around Aaron and said, "Come, make us gods who will go before us. As for this fellow Moses who brought us up out of Egypt, we don't know what has happened to him."

Moses who? It seems from this that the issue was not that God was absent, but God was too slow. It was not that the people of God didn't believe in God. It was that they thought God was working too slow. They grew tired of waiting for God. They liked what God was about. They liked the *idea* of God, but in the mess that was their current situation, they needed something a little more present, something timelier to give them some hope and comfort. *This* is why we caste idols. Because God takes too long! Idols fill the gap of our despair and impatience.

The prophets in Advent come to remind us, though, that our idols are decaying carcasses. Jeremiah spends some thirty chapters making that argument. Then, there is this. Today's scripture is a little oasis, a little drink of water, a little light in the midst of the dark night. Martin Luther called it the little piece of comfort in the sea of shame. Jeremiah finally, *finally*, speaks of something better. [Read Jeremiah 33:14-16.]

Something is sprouting up, says Jeremiah. In a place we thought was nothing but death and sterility, in a place of confusion and desolation, in a place where we thought God had left, left to the terrorists, left to the fascists, left to the narcissist, left to the bullies, in a place and time where we have grown so weary of waiting that we compensate with our own gifts, in this place, finally comes a gift. Finally comes THE gift. No doubt they laughed at him. "Nothing grows from dead wood, Jeremiah! Nothing grows out here in exile. There is nothing righteous here, just corruption and commercialism. You are ridiculous, Jeremiah. You are hopeless." "No," said Jeremiah, "it is righteous." In fact, it is the only righteous thing left, and it will spring up when everything around it seems fake and dead. It is the Advent of Jesus Christ at its own time, on God's own calendar.

See, the real problem is not a "War on Christmas," as some would say, but that Christmas has been stolen by marketplace. More appropriately, the problem is that we have given Christmas to the marketplace long ago, and we will not be getting it back. That doesn't mean that Christ is not at hand. Jeremiah brings prophesy. Jeremiah brings us a promise. Maybe it is hard for us to believe in something so old, something so ancient, so mysterious and spiritual. Maybe it is hard to hear the harsh word from the prophets or the good news when it comes. Maybe all that makes trusting these old promises difficult, but if you ask Jeremiah, he'll tell you that is you are problem. The promise is what it is, and the promise, for those needing translation, is ultimately about a Christ. The promise, in the very words it provides, is about justice for a world that need justice, righteousness for a world that is falling apart, salvation for a world that is dying and safety for a world that is in need of peace. For us who use Christmas to compensate for the world we live in, this is very good news.

Thanks be to God.

Getting Rid of the Tradition
Malachi 3:1-4

See, I am sending my messenger to prepare the way before me, and the Lord whom you seek will suddenly come to his temple. The messenger of the covenant in whom you delight—indeed, he is coming, says the LORD of hosts. ²But who can endure the day of his coming, and who can stand when he appears?

For he is like a refiner's fire and like fullers' soap; ³ he will sit as a refiner and purifier of silver, and he will purify the descendants of Levi and refine them like gold and silver, until they present offerings to the LORD in righteousness. ⁴ Then the offering of Judah and Jerusalem will be pleasing to the LORD as in the days of old and as in former years.

Imagine if you will a holiday party. Logs burn in the fireplace. Garland lines the mantel. The smell of spiced tea wafts through the air. Eggnog is passed around. Neatly wrapped presents are scattered beneath the tree, tagged and fashioned with matching bows. The Carpenters or some holiday standard plays in the background. Friends gather together, arm and arm, to join in the song. It is a happy scene. Until someone takes a hammer to the radio. "Enough already! I'm sick of that song. I'm sick of all of this! It's the same thing every year. Good Gosh! Can't we find something new?!" Everyone is stunned. "What's wrong with him?

This is Malachi. He comes to ruin your Christmas party. He is the second prophet we come to this Advent. His story is the last one you get to in the Old Testament. It is like he has been simmering for pages and then finally explodes. The Malachi story begins in the temple, where he has been coming for years. He comes to temple because he is a faithful child of God. He comes and participates. He comes and watches. He sees the people make their sacrifices, as he has a hundred times. He sees the people pay their alms, as he has a hundred times. He sees the priest offer the prayers, as he has a hundred times. He sees the routine, as he has a hundred times and it about puts him to sleep. It has been done to death. It is tedium to the point of absurdity. Then one day, he just losses it. "Stop it!! Enough already! You are going through the motions! You do it half-heartedly and you've ruined a good thing!" We do not know the reaction. We do not know if people just were shocked or offended. Perhaps they just shrugged their shoulders, "Eeh. You're probably right." Actually, a few verses earlier, the crowd was saying the same thing under their breath. "What a weariness all this is." Malachi, in some ways, is just saying the obvious. He is simply saying what no one else is willing to utter. "Can we sing some *new* songs?"

Of course, usually the answer is "no." "No, we can't sing any new songs. We don't want any new songs. We want the old ones." That's understandable. Christmas is built on tradition. What is Christmas if it isn't Bing Crosby's "White Christmas?" What is it if it isn't the "The Grinch?" What is Christmas if it isn't the trip to Uncle Ed's house on Christmas Eve, as we have done every year since the war; if it isn't the Grandmaw's clam chowder; if it isn't the Maggie's rum cake? Whatever it is. Traditions makes Christmas. It is true in our homes. It is true in our churches: Where we sit. What we sing. What we wear. Tradition is how the past becomes present to us. It is how culture is shared. In keeping traditions, the past becomes present. It is what G.K. Chesterton means when he talks about the "democracy of the dead." Tradition shapes us. It gives us a sense of belonging and history. It allows us to experience something of enduring value. It gives us a sense of home. Tradition makes Christmas ...right up to the point when it gets in the way of it.

Clark Griswold is going to the most wonderful, the most fun-filled old-fashioned family Christmas ever. Sadly, he can't get out of his own way and about blows up his house.[15] Ralphie wants a bb gun and old man Parker wants his traditional turkey dinner. Tragically, the Bumpuses' bloodhounds get loose, storm the kitchen and drag off the dinner[16]. Traditions have a way of ruling our visions, and thus get in the of the very thing we need. We become so beholden to them; we lose sight of the purpose. This is Malachi's point. Can't we sing some *new* songs? Can't we do something *different*? What Malachi knows is this:

---

[15] John Hughes. <u>National Lampoon's Christmas Vacation</u>. Directed by Jeremiah Chechik. (Los Angeles: Warner Brothers, 1989).
[16] Jean Shepherd. <u>A Christmas Story</u>. Directed by Bob Clark. (Los Angeles: MGM/UA, 1983).

Traditions, for all the good about them, can be a big problem. It is true in our homes. It is true in our churches.

For one, traditions exclude. It is hard to break into a group when everyone is speaking a different language and going about a different routine. The new resident wonders why she can't understand it. Traditions also become idolized. They become the sum and substance of the faith. They become the reason, the object. They become the purpose. That is what Jesus railed against. There were about 613 religious laws that need to be followed in order to be righteous. Who can keep up with that? Finally, traditions eventually become shells. People soon begin to simply go through the motions. There is little enthusiasm because no one cares that much anymore. The meaning has been lost. Worshippers forget the deity behind the duty.

As is the case in most of these prophetic moments, God finally steps in and offers God's own perspective. In Malachi, this is what God adds: "Oh, that there were one among you who would shut the doors that you might not kindle another fire upon my altar in vain. I have no pleasure in you, in any of these things. And I will not accept any of this." What God says essentially, is "I'm better than this. I'm better than your half-hearted attempts at faith."

We had a tradition in our family for years. We would go to my grandmother's house for Thanksgiving. We all sat in the same places. She would cook in this big roasting, slow cooker. She would fix this pineapple tort. It was the best. Every year we did this. And then she died. She died three weeks before Thanksgiving in 1977, and we didn't know what to do. I was 10. I assumed there wouldn't be a Thanksgiving because our tradition was dead. I was wrong. My parents decided that we would do something different. We went to the Marriott Hotel and dined at their buffet. To my surprise, we weren't the only people there. To my surprise, it was kind of fun. To my surprise, it ended up being the most memorable Thanksgiving of my childhood. My parents knew what I did not. Thanksgiving was more than a place, a routine or a meal.

The <u>real problem with tradition is that it often excludes the Spirit of God</u>. It is so set in the old that nothing new is getting in. "You hold on to the tradition of man but have left the commandment of God." So, if you want some spiritual renewal at Christmas, don't go back to your ancient routine, no matter how much you think it will make you feel good. If you want some spiritual renewal at Christmas, do not return to your traditions. Dump them. Repent from them. Put yourself into something utterly new, unfamiliar and different.

The Second Sunday of Advent always brings with it a word from John the Baptist. "Repent, the Kingdom of heaven is at hand." That means turn around. Stop doing what you are doing. Do an about face. And old John the Baptist draws from even older Malachi. [Read Malachi 3:1-4]. Christ isn't coming to prop up our past. He is coming to remake us. He is coming to cleanse us. He is coming to save us. And if you don't think the world needs to be saved you haven't been watching the news recently. If you think the passage is a little harsh, think again about last week. The world needs to be dropped in a kiln. It needs a refiner's fire and a fuller's soap. It needs a hard brush to get off the gunk we have acquired. It needs a fire to burn off the darkness and bring forth the clarity, the purity. "We live casual lives," echoes a familiar confession at Advent. "We live casual lives, ignoring God's promised judgment, accepting lies as truth, exploiting neighbors, abusing the earth and refusing God's justice and peace." We DO live casual lives, and we plod carelessly through dated habits.

A friend of mine likens the path of Advent like driving a car to a familiar destination, to "grandmother's house we go." Sometimes in our need for the destination, everything around it becomes "a tradition," the route you take, the car you drive to get there, where people sit in the car, the music you play. Regrettably, if you drive the same way enough, you start falling asleep at the wheel. What Malachi and those like him remind us is that the path through Advent is actually more akin to driving the interstate, in a driving rain, at night, behind three 18-wheelers. All hell is breaking loose around you. You can't see an foot in front of the hood. You have a death grip on your wheel, and you are praying that you make it through ok - whatever route you take, whatever vehicle it takes to get you there. In the Christmas classic, *A Christmas Story*, Old Man Parker threw his turkey carcass on the floor and took the family to a Chinese restaurant for their Christmas dinner.

Curiously, their Christmas turned out just fine, in spite it all. In fact, it didn't come until they did.

The message of Malachi, John the Baptist and the Clark Griswolds of the world is this: We can't keep doing things the same way in our tragic world and think things will just be different. We can't fight the same arguments and beat the same horse again and again. God will one day set this world right. Our job is to turn our hearts, minds, and ways around to Christ and Christ alone. We then look for the day when the lowest of our places are filled up and the highest highs are leveled off and the crooked paths made straight and the rough ways made smooth and all flesh has a clear path to salvation in God Almighty.

Thanks be to God.

Getting Rid of the Arrogance
Zephaniah 3: 14-20

Sing aloud, O daughter Zion; shout, O Israel! Rejoice and exult with all your heart, O daughter Jerusalem! [15] The LORD has taken away the judgments against you, he has turned away your enemies. The king of Israel, the LORD, is in your midst; you shall fear disaster no more. [16] On that day it shall be said to Jerusalem: Do not fear, O Zion; do not let your hands grow weak. [17] The LORD, your God, is in your midst, a warrior who gives victory; he will rejoice over you with gladness, he will renew you in his love; he will exult over you with loud singing [18] as on a day of festival. I will remove disaster from you, [so] that you will not bear reproach for it. [19] I will deal with all your oppressors at that time. And I will save the lame and gather the outcast, and I will change their shame into praise and renown in all the earth. [20] At that time I will bring you home, at the time when I gather you; for I will make you renowned and praised among all the peoples of the earth, when I restore your fortunes before your eyes, says the LORD.

I hope you have picked a side. It is getting late, and it's getting ugly. Oh, we could have predicted it, but it is particularly ugly now. All across our society, it has gotten very ugly. So, go ahead. Pick a side and dig in. Claim the high ground. The other side is. Claim moral integrity. The other side is too. Claim certitude. Everyone else is very sure. Christmas is coming, and we all have to be up in arms. They are coming to take it away. They have no respect for it anymore. They have lost their moral compass. They have wandered from God's path. They are so terrible. And we are so right.

Into the fearful shouting match that is our current culture, into this hot mess, comes the third Sunday of Advent and a word from one more prophet. I realize that when we are so very right, we do not need prophets. We certainly won't listen to them. However, that never stopped a prophet - not one like Zephaniah anyway. The prophet who comes prophesying on this third Sunday of Advent is Zephaniah, Zephaniah Ben Cushi, to be exact. That name, of course, will not do him any favors today. Of course, that would not stop him either. Zephaniah will have his say. He will say his peace. Into raging debate, into fearful shouting match, into hot mess in which sides are so neatly drawn, heels so firmly dug in and everyone is so sure that the other side is the problem, Zephaniah has a word from God. Chapter one, verse 2:

"I will utterly sweep away everything.
I will sweep away man and beast.
I will sweep away birds and fish.
I will overthrow the wicked.
I will cut off mankind."

That's not a nice Christmas message, is it? But Zephaniah would say, "Why do you care about Christmas. You aren't acting like it anyway." Just the verbs are enough to get one's attention. "Sweep away, sweep away, sweep away." Everyone gets caught up in it. There is no good side. There is no bad side. It is just "sweep away, sweep away, sweep away." And then, as soon as a protest or a defense is about to be uttered, there is this: "Be silent. Don't talk. I'll do the talking."

It is funny. On the third Sunday of Advent, this close to Christmas, there is no room for arrogance. There is no room for false piety, for religious pretense, for moral hubris. Stop it. Be silent. For no one is any better in this world than anyone else. "All have sinned and fallen short," someone would say sometime later. "Sweep away, sweep away, sweep away." It is a harsh message. It was then. For the Israelites who first heard the prophet, they had to be a little stunned. If you read all of Zephaniah (it isn't long), you will notice that he starts knocking off every group, one by one: Philistines, Moabites, Ammonites, Assyrians, Ethiopians, Cherethites, Ashkelonites, and then, Jerusalem. No one is above the sweeping. All have sinned and fallen short.

That is hard to hear. Nonetheless, it IS the message that arrives before Christ comes. John the Baptist shows up in the Gospel of Luke. No one is safe from him either. "You brood of vipers!" He says this to everyone, including all these faithful children of God who just knew they were in the right. They were sons and daughters of Abraham, for goodness sake! "You brood of vipers. Bear some fruit worthy of repentance!" Like Zephaniah, he had a list too. "Who? Who should repent, John? Tax Collectors?" "Yes." "Soldiers?" "Yes." Everyone.

No one is above the sweeping. All have sinned and fallen short. Everyone. Everyone on all sides of any dividing line.

That ought to create a bit of humility, should it not? But, boy, humility is in rare supply these days. You know, in our culture today, there is all kinds of confusion about all kinds of things, all kinds of dividing lines. Now there is even great confusion around Christmas. What it is? What it isn't? Who celebrates it? Who doesn't it? Our society has become more secular, more pluralistic. Still, even in this climate, Christmas seems to have grown. Everyone, it seems, celebrates Christmas, even if they do not celebrate the Christ. This creates a lot controversy. It creates conflict. Christians long ago left Christmas to culture. It isn't coming back now. Culture claims Christmas, even if it doesn't always claim the Christ. Sadly, what has become a perfect opportunity to witness to the Gospel is often abandoned in Christian hostility, defensiveness and judgment. "Jesus is the reason for the season," we shout. We shout it louder and louder, with great seriousness and anger. "Jesus is the reason! Jesus is the reason!" After a while, others only notice our shouting and not our message.

Reflecting on the arms race of the 70s and 70s, Richard Nixon, of all people, said that "America needed to be careful for America would destroy its freedom in attempting to defend it."[17] What he meant is that we often sabotage our own purposes in careless attempts at defending our purpose. The same could be said for many things. We would destroy our faith in attempting to defend it. We would destroy Christmas in attempting to defend it.

Saleh Murtaja owns a gift shop in Gaza. Among many other items, he sells Christmas trees. In the last few years, though, he has noticed a shift in his market. He is selling Christmas trees to Muslims. This is bizarre. Last year, he sold as many to Muslims as he did to Christians.[18]

---

[17] Richard Dean Burns and Joseph M Siracusa. *Global History of the Nuclear Arms Race: Weapons, Strategy, and Politics.* (Santa Barbara, CA: Praeger, 2013).

[18] Asmaa al-Ghoul, Muslims Joins Christians for Christmas Celebrations in Gaza. http://www.al-monitor.com/pulse/originals/2014/12/christmas-gaza-muslims-christians-celebrate-remember-war.html#

Now, this hardly makes sense, but it is happening. Of course, this is not without controversy. There are sides, you know. Some of the Christians are angry that he is allowing Muslims to buy them because Christmas is a Christian holiday. Some of the Muslims are angry that he is selling them to Muslims and think he is trying to propagate the Christian faith. Some of the Muslims are angry and want to chop off the heads of the Muslims who bought the trees. Some of the Christians are angry that he is selling trees to Christians because Christmas celebrations are not spelled out in Scripture and therefore unbiblical and really un-Christian. Some Christians are angry because the trees are plastic and come from China. Saleh doesn't care. He is glad to sell as many trees as he can. Saleh is a business owner and wants to make a buck. Sometimes the marketplace is the great leveler. In spite it all, Saleh comes out ahead. And so, by the way, does Jesus.

We don't control Christmas. We never have. We don't need to defend Christmas. It isn't ours to defend. Christmas isn't ours to bring about. It doesn't need our help. Christmas comes regardless of us, regardless of anyone. Christmas comes as it always has; by the hand of God and in the gift of a child. Christmas is now no longer an exclusive Christian holiday, but maybe God's hand is in that too.

Nothing can cure one's arrogance like a child. A child will make you look stupid, in front of the world. Your child, your kid, will make it their pleasure to bring you back down to earth. This is because arrogance rises from control. With the illusion of control, with the illusion of certitude, comes arrogance. Once we realize we have no control, once we realize how little we know, suddenly we are not that arrogant. Everyone is great at parenting a child until they actually have one. From the first day, babies have a way of displacing our control. You can plan all you want, but a baby will come when and where the baby wants to come. Nine months is always exactly nine months. Oh, sure you can plan a c-section, but even with that, the child is going to have some say. That is how it is with any baby, including the one that comes on Christmas Eve. We don't control Jesus. We can't contain his message, his way. We certainly don't get to determine who and where it rises. We have very little control over anything. We have no reason us.

The other thing about babies, though, is that, generally, they bring with them great joy. Watch a room when someone walks in with a baby. Watch the family when a baby is born. Watch in worship when we baptize an infant. People sleep through sermons, stand silent during hymns, pass notes during prayers. A baptism? Everyone is paying attention. Babies bring joy. And so it is with the one that comes in 11 days. What is the first pronouncement about that baby? "Good tidings of great *joy*."

Today's Zephaniah scripture comes from the end of the book that bears his name. Finally, after so much sweeping, something promising is uttered. In that day, says the prophet, the oppressors will be gone, the wicked will be gone, the disasters will be gone and all those that caused you fear will be gone. Moreover, the lame will be saved, the refugees will be gathered in, the shamed shall be praised, the lost arrive home, the scattered are gathered together and the fortunes are restored. Do you hear the relief in this passage? Do you hear the joy? That is what the babe in the manager brings.

Zephaniah says this at one point:

> *"At that time, I will change the speech of people to a pure speech.*
>
> *Then all of them may call on the name of the Lord and serve him with one accord.*
>
> *From beyond the rivers of Ethiopia, my suppliants will bring my offering.*
>
> *On that day, you shall not be put to shame anymore because of the deeds by which you have rebelled against me, for then I will remove from your midst your proud exalted ones and you shall no longer be haughty in my holy mountain.*
>
> *For I will leave in the midst of you, a people, humble and lowly."*

If you want some spiritual renewal this Christmas, give up your confidence. Give up your control. Give up your arrogance. Give INTO joy. Enjoy this strange phenomenon that all these people are drawn to the light of Christmas even if they are not yet quite sure why.

Thanks be to God.

Counted

Luke 2

In those days a decree went out from Emperor Augustus that all the world should be registered. ²This was the first registration and was taken while Quirinius was governor of Syria. ³All went to their own towns to be registered. ⁴Joseph also went from the town of Nazareth in Galilee to Judea, to the city of David called Bethlehem, because he was descended from the house and family of David. ⁵He went to be registered with Mary, to whom he was engaged and who was expecting a child. ⁶While they were there, the time came for her to deliver her child. ⁷And she gave birth to her firstborn son and wrapped him in bands of cloth, and laid him in a manger, because there was no place for them in the inn.

⁸In that region there were shepherds living in the fields, keeping watch over their flock by night. ⁹Then an angel of the Lord stood before them, and the glory of the Lord shone around them, and they were terrified. ¹⁰But the angel said to them, "Do not be afraid; for see—I am bringing you good news of great joy for all the people: ¹¹to you is born this day in the city of David a Savior, who is the Messiah, the Lord. ¹²This will be a sign for you: you will find a child wrapped in bands of cloth and lying in a manger." ¹³And suddenly there was with the angel a multitude of the heavenly host, praising God and saying, ¹⁴"Glory to God in the highest heaven, and on earth peace among those whom he favors!"

Christmas begins not with candlelight and poinsettias. It begins not with joyful cantatas or even quiet peacefulness. Christmas begins in tedium. Caesar wants an accounting. He wants to know how many people he has under his rule. So everybody goes back home to pencil in their bubble sheet on how many people live in their household. Christmas begins in tedium. Tedium with a taste of fear. Because when emperors start counting people, it usually is a bad sign. When emperors start counting the number of minorities they have, particularly when they start numbering their Jewish minorities, something terrible is going to happen. Such is the case in the Bible. On Christmas, when everybody has to be registered. In fact, emperor demonstrates a bit of an ego, when he declares that the "whole world should be registered!" And so, everybody who is anybody must be counted. And this is where Christmas begins. This is where Christmas is born. In a world where everyone is marked, labeled, categorized, valued and documented.

You are an object. A unit. A population. A demographic. A market. A deduction. An expense. A percentage. A statistic. A number. And so there they all go, Joseph, Mary and all the rest, marching obediently to their legal residence where they can be documented. All of them. "All went to their own towns to be registered," says Luke. Well… not to debate Scripture, but that is not exactly true. Not all of them went. The shepherds, you may recall, didn't go. While everyone else was packing up, loading up, trekking across the country to their respective towns to take care of the empire's business, shepherds stayed right where they were, "living in the field, keeping watch over their flocks by night."

I'm not sure why they didn't go. Maybe they didn't get the emails (not much service in the fields). Maybe they turned in absentee ballots. But much more likely, they didn't need to be counted because they didn't count.

Now, we know that shepherds were not widely valued. Menial work. Low pay. Bad hours. Messy job. Shiftless population. No one thought much of shepherds. No one could name one decent one… except David of course. Even the empire, which demands an accounting of everything, didn't think enough of the shepherds to count them. They were not held in high esteem. So, while everyone else is getting back home before Christmas, filling out their forms and taking care of their business, the shepherds are still out living under the stars. They might be well be living out of a yellow school bus at the Walmart. This is where Christmas is born.

I sometimes wonder why people come to church on Christmas Eve. I wonder sometimes if they come to be counted. Just as sometimes we come to be seen and to see, I wonder if we come to be counted - to say we have been here, to do what we have always done, to do what we are supposed to do, to do what we are asked to do. I wonder sometimes why so many people come on Christmas Eve. I wonder what they are looking for. I wonder if the candlelight is really worth the packed pews and the noisy nave. I wonder what we are all looking for and what we actually find. After we have counted all that we need for Christmas. After we have been counted for everything we are needed for, after we have been sized up, taxed and categorized, after our office parties and teacher conferences, after being filling our gas tanks or filing through TSAs, we all end up here, waiting for the story of the angels.

But, of course, the angels don't come to us first. They come first to the ones who are not counted. They come first to the shepherds. Fittingly for the Gospel of Luke, it is on the wings of angels that good news comes to the all the earth, and they come first to the unaccounted-for shepherds living in the fields keeping watch over their flock by night. The multitude concludes their announcement with this now famous praise:

> *"Glory to God in the highest heaven,*
> *and peace on the earth among those whom he favors!"*

Have you ever thought about that praise? Have you ever wondered about it, particularly that last part?

> *"Peace on the earth among those whom he favors!"*

Do you ever wonder who exactly it is that he favors? What does that actually mean? Some scholars interpret it as a phrase of emotion. May peace rest upon the earth, among us, for he favors us, he loves us. That makes sense. "God so loved the world he gave his only son." Other scholars interpret it as a phrase of will.[19] May peace rest upon the earth, among only the people he favors, the ones he chooses. Though this might feel rather exclusive to us, it is in keeping with sense of divine election. One has to be careful here because people for years have battled about who it is, they think God favors. Curiously, everyone who argues for this interpretation is conveniently in the group God happens to favor!

Now, I take a little bit of both of them. I tend to think God's blessings always reach farther than our own biases. But if you want to read this scripture rather literally, if you want to put a tight election on the phrase "those whom God favors," then, based on the scripture, God favors the shepherds. They are the ones who get the greeting.

---

[19] Francois Bovon, <u>A Commentary on Luke 1:1 - 9:50</u>. (Philadelphia: Fortress Press, 2002).

This is an important point on Christmas Eve, if a difficult one. Christmas comes first to the unworthy, undocumented and unaccounted for. In the words of one scholar, "It is clear that Christ came to be savior for all persons, rich and poor, alike but it is also equally clear that God chose to dwell among the least and the lost. And comes first to them."[20] So, if you want a bit of the peace that comes at Christmas then one option is to seek out the "unworthy, undocumented and unaccounted for," to see what kind of reception they are getting today and to ask how we might be among the faithful who receive them, regardless of risk. That is one way. Another way is to tap into the piece of you that is unworthy, undocumented and unaccounted for. If you are seeking that peace that comes at Christmas, tap into that place, even if you think you are somebody, even if you are one of those whose gets a number by your name or a letter behind it, even if you are someone who counts. If you want to share in the rejoicing, you have to find that part of you that desperately needs a savior.

In this world, you are just a number. Just like Mary and Joseph and the rest, a cog, a vote, a position, a market, a subscriber, a statistic. You are a number. But here at the manger, you are favored. Unworthy though you may be in all truthfulness. Nonetheless, at the manger, you are not a number, you are part of "all people." And we, we have been gifted. A savior has been born to us. This world has few purposes for you. To count you. To capture you. To kill you. To count you for their records, for their documents, for their registrations. To capture you for some purpose, for your vote, your wallet, for their bottom line, their product. To kill you because you are there. Into such a world, comes a God that lives and dies for you.

Consider this: In a world that would kill children, God comes to us as a child. We are here tonight because we know that while we count for nothing, God loves us. We are here tonight because we know that while we count for nothing, God loves us enough to come in all vulnerability and to live and die for us.

---

[20] Robert Redman in <u>Feasting on the Word</u>, Year C, Volume 1, David L Bartlett and Barbara Brown Taylor, editors. (Louisville: WJKP, 2009).

Glory to God on the highest
And on earth peace among all us unworthy people with him he is pleased.

Thanks be to God.

Out of Egypt
Matthew 2:13-23

Have you ever noticed that the news doesn't change on the Sunday after Christmas? On Christmas Eve, we had a nice service. The sanctuary was filled with worshipers. We heard again the ancient Christmas story, foretold by prophets and proclaimed by Gospel writers. We shared the holy sacrament. Then, with lit candles, we processed outside where the mass of worshipers gathered silently as we have done for many generations and sang. "Silent night, holy night. All is calm, all is bright." The music and lyrics remind us of the peace we celebrate, of the good news of the world. Yes, there is terror, warfare and disease. Yes, there are tornadoes, earthquakes and typhoons. Yes, there is fear and dread. Still "unto us a child is born and to us a Son is given."

But the Sunday after Christmas, all the news is the same. The headlines didn't change. It is like the world didn't get the message of the angels. On the Sunday after Christmas, the news picks up where it left off. Yes, 'to us a child is born and to us a Son is given,' but there are still tornados, earthquakes and typhoons. There is still terror, still warfare and still disease. One cannot help but wonder if the whole baby Jesus story is but a respite, an interlude to an otherwise noisy world.

Scripture, by the way, reflects that same painful reality. Christmas Eve we read of the sweet story of Mary and the baby. We read of the simple manger and the gentle shepherds with tender sheep. We hear about kings who come from afar, who come with all their exotic mystery to worship the child. It is lovely. On the Sunday after Christmas, though, Herod shows up. Who are these people who think Holy Scripture doesn't reflect reality? This is just like the world, isn't it? It is the Sunday after Christmas and Herod is knocking at the door. The world goes right on being the world in spite of the sweet baby in the manger.

The baby's parents have three sets of visitors who want to pay them a visit. The first two groups we love to tell about on Christmas Eve. The third group, Herod's group, we generally wait until the Sunday after Christmas to talk about them. There is a word on the street. Herod is angry. Herod is angry because the wise men didn't come back like they agreed. They saw through Herod's deception and went home by another way, circumventing the king. Kings don't like to be circumvented. They don't like to be made to look foolish. Not any king, and certainly not THIS king. Certainly not Herod. So Herod is angry, and Herod wants this child. He doesn't like the sound of a messiah being born in his kingdom. He doesn't like the idea of some child being king. He doesn't like this Jesus. He wants rid of this Jesus, and what the king wants the king gets.

You will notice that this is no targeted manhunt. Herod isn't sending out a special operations unit to slid across the ground in the cover of night. No, it is much more of a blanket bombing campaign. "Let's just kill all the male children 2 years and under. That way we will be sure to get him." That is how kings operate. That is how our world operates. No, the Sunday after Christmas is not Christmas. It is like every other day of the year. There may be no more of an honest scripture than this one.

After Christmas, things get back to normal. Take the cute wreath off the car. We can get the wise men back to planning how to build a bomb. We can send the shepherds back to their minimum wage jobs so we can make fun of how they talk. We can get this baby Jesus out of the town because the last thing we need in our land is another refugee family looking for shelter. After Christmas, the world goes back to be the world. After Christmas, after the cute little candlelight services are over and after everybody gets their fill of warm fuzzies, we can all go back to cruelty that is our world.

But even though we are so very used to it, it can be discouraging. For that reason, I want to do something differently today. I want to remind you of your split personality, your own dual nature.

See, I have come to believe that we participate in two narratives. What I mean by this is there is the narrative of what we see and know to be true about living in the world. It is influenced by our culture and our economy, by the winds and rains. It is a narrative primarily of a basic understanding, albeit often cynical, of the world and how life is, of damned-if you do and damned-if you don't, of helplessness and fear, of the strong survive and sometimes not even them. We also, though, participate in another narrative. Because of our baptisms or because of our confession of faith or just because we choose to show up each Sunday wondering if there is something of importance here, we participate in a narrative of faith. We participate in a narrative that tells us that there is something more than what we see. This narrative is about a greater truth. It affirms a way we do not always notice, but one in which our all hopes and fears ultimately rest.

We participate in the narrative of our world because we have to. Not to do so would be to be dangerous and naive. We participate in the narrative of our faith because it is the only thing that can sustain us. We would perish otherwise. Sometimes, often times, of course, the narratives clash. The world narrative is hard and concrete. It is full tilt. It is loud and crashing. The faith narrative, however, is rather … quiet. That is part of its trouble. That is what makes it hard to believe. It seems particularly vulnerable.

Everyone is hollering that this child is the Messiah, the chosen one, the one to save us, but the world seems to have its way with this young child. King Herod is killing babies like he must eat burgers. And little homeless Jesus is shuffled around like a bag of dirty hush money. He's in Bethlehem. No, he's in Egypt. No, he's back in Israel. No, in Galilee, in Nazareth! It's like searching for Waldo. How much of a "deliverer" can he be when he keeps being shipped about? He's not delivering. He's being delivered!

After a brief respite, after a pretty Christmas, things get back to normal. The narrative of the world seems too loud not to notice. Yet, if you are going to participate in two narratives, you have to know a few things. One, is that you have to be bilingual. You have to be able to read two languages. The narrative of the world, of course, uses the language of kings. The narrative of faith, however, uses the language of infants. Also, if you are going to participate in two narratives, you also have to know that the two narratives have different ways of producing their stories. They will work them out in different ways. Even as the narrative of the world seems to be making great headway, the narrative of faith seems to find other ways, subversive ways, to emerge.

In the days after 9/11, many stories emerged as well. Stories of fear. Stories of faith. One such story sticks with me to this day. Apparently, as people tried to escape the cloud of rubble of the two collapsing towers, many, hundreds even, took refuge in the historic Trinity Church of lower Manhattan. Covered in grey ash from head to toe, one couldn't tell who was white and who was black, who was a Wall Street investor or a Wall street vender. But the story goes that many made their way to the one place where they could get clean. The priest grabbed the baptismal fount and started cleaning out eyes so the blinded could see. He had to clean out their eyes with baptismal water because it was readily available. Otherwise, the only thing they would see would be ash.

Now, in the narrative of the world this is a nice story, a story of a kind man performing a helpful act with the closest available cleaning liquid. In the narrative of faith, however, is it something much more. It becomes a story with layers of meaning - of the ashes and dirt we all one day return to, of the baptismal waters that give us life and allow us to see in spite of the death and of the Good Samaritans we meet along the way. One event. Two narratives. One narrative is a matter of fact. The other is a matter of faith that draws you to deeper meaning.

If you have a Bible in front of you, look again at Matthew 2:13-23 The most powerful verse in the scripture, for me, is this one:

> *"A voice is heard in Ramah, wailing and loud lamentation,*
> *Rachel weeping for her children;*
> *She refused to be consoled, because they are no more."*

There in the midst of this unsettling story of Herod massacring thousands of infants is suddenly this passage drawn from the book of Jeremiah. It's placement in the gospel is meant to connect the people of God to a similar horror that happened to them generations earlier. The purpose is to connect the present grief surrounding Herod's atrocity with a similar grief surrounding Rachel of Old Testament days. The Scripture is Jeremiah 31:15. It is a brutal piece of scripture, raw in its emotion, very present in its pain.

The story of Ramah is a sad one. Ramah is a city of exile, a place where, once again, God's promise for Israel is at risk. Rachel, as some of us remember, is the mother of 12 children, twelve children which translate into the 12 tribes of Israel. And with their death goes God's promise of Israel's future, Israel's posterity. So, Rachel cries. Rachel laments. She will not be consoled. You can try to console her, but she will push you away. She wants none of your helpless help. Her grief is very, very deep. Rachel weeps for her children. And Rachel also weeps because their death is an indication of the death of God's very promise. So the Jeremiah passage deepens the level of despair in this post-Christmas story.

> *"A voice is heard in Ramah,*
> *wailing and loud lamentation,*
> *Rachel weeping for her children;*
> *she refused to be consoled, because they are no more."*

And it is not a big leap to allow the same passage to speak to any contemporary situation. "A voice is heard in Ramah,

> A voice is heard in lower Manhattan,
> A voice is heard in Newtown,
> A voice is heard is heard in Charleston and Charlottesville,
>   and Atlanta and Richmond,
>   And Manteo and Murphy and Raleigh and Wilson.
> Wailing and loud lamentation,
> Rachel is weeping for her children.
> She refuses to be consoled,
> Because they are no more."

This, of course, is the narrative of our world, with one more tragedy to offer. But I will tell you, there something hidden in Matthew's gospel There is something subversive happening. Matthew doesn't give you all of Jeremiah chapter 31. He only gives you part of it. I think he does this intentionally. Perhaps because he wants us to find it ourselves. Perhaps because he thinks we might remember it. In any case, there is more to the Jeremiah Rachel story. It is hidden in the text. The rest of the Jeremiah text goes like this…
[Jeremiah 31:15]

"A voice is heard in Ramah,
wailing and loud lamentation,
Rachel weeping for her children;
She refused to be consoled, because they are no more."

[Jeremiah 31:16:]

"But thus says the Lord;
Keep your voice from weeping,
and your eyes from tears,
For your work shall be rewarded," says the Lord.
They shall come back from the land of their enemy.
There is hope for your future and
Your children shall come back to their own country."

Matthew doesn't give us that part, does he? That beautiful, powerful, holy, awesome proclamation of the Lord is hidden beneath the words of Matthew, hidden under the narrative of this world. And those who are willing to work through the hard layers might find it. This word of hope is not apparent in the Scripture. It is not apparent in the world either, certainly not after Christmas, but it is there, if only slightly buried.

After a pretty Christmas, things will seem to get back to normal. The narrative of the world will be at full tilt. Bethlehem will go back to the bombs that leave it always desolate. But do not be deceived. We participate in TWO narratives. One remains hidden, working itself out in quiet, subversive, other-worldly ways.

You know, you could argue that today's scripture is about the world and its cruel narrative. You could argue that today's scripture is essentially about Herod and Herod's cruel ways. He is the one with all the power in the story. He is the one that everyone is afraid of. He is the one that everyone is listening to and taking cues from. He is the one making things happen. He is the one who has the most quotations. And any time you see quotation marks in Scripture, you know that individual has power. Herod has all kinds of words, all kinds of narrative force. He thusly has all kinds of power. Jesus, on the contrary, has none. Jesus says not one word. You remember: "not even crying he makes." Herod is the force. Herod is the narrative. But curiously, at the end of the passage, Herod is also dead. Isn't that interesting? For all his force, for all his posturing, for all his bravado and power, for all this threat of death and murder, at the end of the story, quite ironically, the one who demanded death is the one who is dead! And seemingly powerless baby Jesus, is alive and well. It makes you wonder what other power might be in play, doesn't it?

It is the Sunday after Christmas and the world are the same. The world is full of Herods and it scares the hell out of us. Certainly, it is best to wise to them. They are dangerous. But do not forget there is another story at work in this world. You may not always see it or recognize it at first glance, but it is there. And it is there that the hopes and fears of all the world are met.

Thanks be to God.

Crisis in Gethsemane
Mark 14: 32-42

Over the next few weeks of Lent, we will be looking closely at the events of Jesus' life leading up to his death. More specifically, we are going to spend the next five weeks on two days of Scripture. A great deal happens in those two days, a lot that rarely finds a Sunday pulpit because of standard lectionary readings. This will be our focus.

They went to a place called Gethsemane; and he said to his disciples, "Sit here while I pray." [33] He took with him Peter and James and John and began to be distressed and agitated. [34] And he said to them, "I am deeply grieved, even to death; remain here, and keep awake." [35] And going a little farther, he threw himself on the ground and prayed that, if it were possible, the hour might pass from him. [36] He said, "Abba, Father, for you all things are possible; remove this cup from me; yet, not what I want, but what you want." [37] He came and found them sleeping; and he said to Peter, "Simon, are you asleep? Could you not keep awake one hour? [38] Keep awake and pray that you may not come into the time of trial; the spirit indeed is willing, but the flesh is weak." [39] And again he went away and prayed, saying the same words. [40] And once more he came and found them sleeping, for their eyes were very heavy; and they did not know what to say to him. [41] He came a third time and said to them, "Are you still sleeping and taking your rest? Enough! The hour has come; the Son of Man is betrayed into the hands of sinners. [42] Get up, let us be going. See, my betrayer is at hand."

Jesus seems rather annoyed, doesn't he? You can't blame him. He has to be extremely stressed. The scriptures tell you as much "Distressed. Agitated. Deeply grieved." He led them to the Mount of Olives, which apparently was a common site to which grieving people returned. People since the time of King David climbed up that hillside to find some quiet alone space among the olive trees to grieve.[21] Jesus apparently did so before.[22]

They finish their last supper. They move up to the Mt of Olives. He tells the disciples to sit down and wait while he goes to pray. He already

---

[21] 2 Sam 15.20
[22] See Gospel of Luke

explained what was to happen to him. They have to know he is beside-himself. "Sit here and wait. Stay awake. Do that much for me." He goes off, falls to the ground and prays the most heart-wrenching prayer ever uttered from his lips. What do the disciples do? They nap. Jesus comes back and finds them napping. Napping. "Simon are you asleep?" he asks incredulously. "You can't stay awake an hour?"

Jesus is not asking them to do any real heavy lifting. He didn't make them walk as far as he walked up that mountain. He didn't even ask them to pray (Heaven forbid they might offer a prayer). No, he simply asked that they stay awake. Why? So they could watch out for Romans coming to arrest him? So that they might be attentive to the events around them? So that they might at the very least show some support? Whatever the reason they can't stay up. It was a long day. They just had a few glasses of wine at last supper. Who knows? Whatever the reason, they fall asleep, and they do so just moments after they just promised to stick with Jesus to the bitter end. Ironic, isn't it? Jesus says, "You will all fall away." Simon Peter then protest. "Not me, Lord! I'll follow you to my own life's end! I'll never deny you! I'll never abandon you in your time of need!" Four short verses later and he's sound asleep. Kind of sad, isn't it? Kind of embarrassing, isn't it?

What a difference a word makes... even a few words. In my mind Jesus' words are offered for a reason. He tells them to "sit here while I pray." He didn't tell them to "stay here" or "wait here" or "stand here." He specifically, in the Greek, says "sit." In most every case when a rabbi says "sit" to his students, there is a teaching that is going to take place. It is the model of teaching that was used. So, in my mind, when Jesus tells them to "sit," for whatever else is going on, he is using this opportunity to teach these disciples one more lesson. His world may be coming down around him. The hand of God might be on him and on this world in a particular way never before known, but in Jesus' mind, it is still an opportunity to teach.

I've been with people in their dying. Many of you have too. It is not unusual in those moments to realize that, even as you are grieving, you are also learning something, you are being taught something about life and death. In those moment, you learn from the person you are losing. It is true. In a similar but even more profound way, something like that is happening here. "Sit. Wait. Stay alert. Watch. Keep awake." Jesus wants them to learn something. Yet, they don't. They take a nap instead. Thank heavens for Mark. For in the providential ways of God's purpose, we at least get to witness the lesson. We at least get to hear his prayer, if we can't stomach it. Like being a witness to someone else's suffering, this is difficult to look upon.

We see an emotional man. That is hard to see. Jesus is angry. He is sad. He is annoyed. He calls out to God, using a very personal name for Father. He calls Peter by name, the only time in Mark he calls anyone by name directly. Jesus is emotionally all over the place. We also see a grieving man. That is hard to witness. It is not easy to look on a grieving man. The fact that it is Jesus, our messiah, who is this emotional, this grieving, is difficult. So difficult, by the way, that some ancient scholars have tried to dismiss it or explain it away. John Calvin would have none of that. "There are a few new stoics today, who count it depraved not only to groan and weep, but even to be sad. We (shall) have nothing to do with this iron philosophy which our Lord and Master has condemned, not only by his word, but also by his example. For he groaned and he wept."[23]

We also see in Jesus a conflicted man. This might be the most problematic. Jesus isn't supposed to be conflicted, but there it is, in black and white. He prayed that this hour might "pass from him." He prayed that the Lord remove this cup from him. And then a "yet." "Yet, not my will but your will." Jesus is conflicted. So if an emotional messiah is hard to stomach, so much more is a conflicted one. Again, people for years have tried to explain this one away. "Oh, he really doesn't mean it. He really didn't feel that way or think that way." Really? Because that what he says. "Oh, he really didn't want to avoid the death." Really? Because he sure is praying for it. And why would he pray for it to be removed if he didn't want it to be removed. Why else is he deeply agitated, grieved and falling on the ground? He is conflicted man. This is hard to get one's mind around.

We see an emotional man, grieving, conflicted man. And certainly we see a lonely man. Jesus is a very lonely man. That too is hard to hear, but he is. Everyone deserts him, even his closest friends and allies.

---

[23] John Calvin, Institutes, 3.8.9

They can't even stand watch for him. He is very lonely. That happens in grief, though, doesn't it? Even when we know other people have gone through grief, even when we know other people feel badly for us, even when we know other people might be going through the same thing, it is lonely. When we are in grief, it is exceptionally isolating. Perhaps it is even more so for Jesus, who is about to take this walk to the cross all by himself.

There can be no doubt that Jesus is all these things, that he prays a lonely, emotional, conflicted prayer. I think, though, that is part of the lesson. Beyond whatever important things the prayer tells us about the nature of Jesus as fully human and fully divine, and beyond whatever important things it shows us about the working of God's purpose in the world, the prayer is, for those who sit and stay awake, a lesson for those others falling to the ground, for those collapsing under the weight of their own grief. For anyone else who climb up to their own Mt Olives to hide away in prayer of distress or to break down in confusion of purpose Jesus shows you how to do it.

"Abba, Father, for you all things are possible. Remove this cup from me. Yet not what I want but what you want." Jesus calls God by every name in his book, calling him father in both Greek and Aramaic. He then he prays a prayer that is both soul bearing and faith endearing. Now, in my mind, there is an A portion of this prayer and a B portion of this prayer. The A portion is the soul bearing. It is the plea. It is his deep desire. It is what he wants, what he cries for. It is heartfelt and honest. It is pure humanity. Then there is the B portion of the prayer. The B portion is the faith endearing. It is the letting go and the trusting in what cannot be seen. It is the putting your life, your hopes and fears in God's hands. It is the act of submission and contrition. It is allowing your heart to be tended to by the invisible heart of God. It is to trust that there is a great purpose at play and that, though things may not end up as you wish, in the end, God's purpose will be done, and your concerns will be taken up in the will and love of the Father. There is A portion and a B portion: A - "Remove this cup." B -" Yet not what I want but what you want."

An A and B. Jesus prays them both. The disciples, by the way, pray neither. They fail on both counts. They certainly don't trust the Father with what going to happen. But they also can't be honest enough to offer an honest prayer. They are just full of bravado and self-confidence. Jesus, once again, does what they cannot do, both in terms of him being divine, but also in terms of him being human. The prayer, that unique balance of A and B in a crisis on Gethsemane, is instructive for anyone walking up that mountain of despair.

Some people are quick to pray the "B" portion, the "not my will but Thy will" prayer. They never offer the A portion. That would be too much. That would be too harsh or too emotional. They are just so good they go right to the B. These are Doris Day Christians. "Whatever will be will be!" Now, it might seem faithful, but it is honestly a little less than honest, isn't it? After all, who is more insufferable than Christians who appear not to suffer anything? A "B' prayer without any "A" comes across naive at best and dispassionate at worse. Thank God for a Christ who prays nothing like that.

On the other end, there are those who pray the "A" portion and never get to the "B." They are good at the "remove the cup," but are not so good at the "not what I want but what you want." Quite honestly, this is most the people I know. It is hard not to be that way. Yet, if you are honest, unless you at least make an attempt at getting to B, your suffering is unresolved. A without B is an unresolved life which never gets better. A and B. B without A is hallowing and dishonest. A without B is despairing and close-minded. But together, it works. B allows one to trust that the end is secure in Gods' will. A allows one to know one's voice is heard. There has to be both. No doubt, it is hard to witness and hard to listen to, but it is honest and faithful. Many a person has climbed up to their own Mt Olive and fallen before God in grief. Thanks be to God that there is an invitation to prayer that is both life-wrenchingly honest and other-worldly trusting. There is a lesson here for sure, for those willing to sit and stay awake.

I used to be annoyed at those disciples who couldn't stay awake for Jesus in his time of need. I used to mock them. Then I turned 50. I sit down in a comfortable chair at the end of a day, and I'm asleep in three minutes. Sometimes you just can't help yourself. You want to stay away, but you can't. You are driving down a road at night and you get sleepy. You know if you fall asleep you will likely crash and die. Still, your head starts nodding and your eyes get heavy. You don't want to. You can't help it!

We are like that in so many ways. The very things we don't want to do, we do. The very things we do want to do, we don't. Long ago, someone saw that quality in humans and called it "sin." That quality forever prevents us from being the kind of people we should be or having the world we desire. Thank God our salvation is not dependent on our ability to stay awake or to successfully pray or even to always abide close to Jesus. Thank God our salvation is not dependent on our ability to be honest. Our salvation hinges on one who is, though. In Christ, we see one who can unload his heart to the Father and trust the Father with it. That should get our attention enough to sit up and take notice, that there remains one place to leave our trials and our trust.

Thanks be to God.

Betrayed with a Kiss
Mark 14: 10-11, 43-50

Then Judas Iscariot, who was one of the twelve, went to the chief priests in order to betray him to them. ¹¹ When they heard it, they were greatly pleased, and promised to give him money. So he began to look for an opportunity to betray him.

Immediately, while he was still speaking, Judas, one of the twelve, arrived; and with him there was a crowd with swords and clubs, from the chief priests, the scribes, and the elders. ⁴⁴ Now the betrayer had given them a sign, saying, "The one I will kiss is the man; arrest him and lead him away under guard." ⁴⁵ So when he came, he went up to him at once and said, "Rabbi!" and kissed him. ⁴⁶ Then they laid hands on him and arrested him. ⁴⁷ But one of those who stood near drew his sword and struck the slave of the high priest, cutting off his ear. ⁴⁸ Then Jesus said to them, "Have you come out with swords and clubs to arrest me as though I were a bandit? ⁴⁹ Day after day I was with you in the temple teaching, and you did not arrest me. But let the scriptures be fulfilled." ⁵⁰ All of them deserted him and fled.

Eleven years ago, when Julie and I were thinking of names for the son who was about to born, we considered many options. We liked the name Henry, but we had a dog named Henry and for some reason Julie didn't want to name our son after a dog. We eventually, of course, settled on "Jack." Of the many options for names, though, "Judas" was not one of them. We did not once consider the name Judas.

Nobody names their child Judas anymore, do they? Judas never quite makes the list of most popular children names. Is there a more hated person in Scripture? Judas. The Betrayer. He sold out Jesus. He hung him out to dry. He turned him over to the chief priests and their henchmen. He betrayed him. For all the blame cast about after Jesus' crucifixion, for all the finger-pointing at the Roman soldiers, at the Roman leadership, at the Pharisees and the chief priests, eventually it comes back to Judas.

"The chief priests and scribes were looking for a way to arrest Jesus by stealth," reads the Scripture. They never did, though, until someone knocked on their door. Judas knocked on their door. "Judas went to the chief priest in order to betray him." Judas went to them. They didn't approach him. He approached them. For all the blame-casting about crucifixion, it was Judas who got the ball rolling. Actually, that isn't exactly what the scripture says. It says, "Judas, one of the twelve, went to the chief priest in order to betray him." One of the twelve. That is what is so painful and so critical. For all the blame-casting about the crucifixion, it was "one of the twelve" who initiated the process of crucifying Jesus. Let that sink in. It was the *church* who initiated the process of crucifying Jesus Christ.

No wonder we hate Judas. Certainly, this is a very personal thing for the church. For Romans and chief priests, they don't care. For them, Judas is simply an informant. For the empire, Judas is just the witness who can identify Jesus in the police line-up. He is just the one who points him out. For the church, though, he is a betrayer. That is his name now. "The Betrayer." Not "The Rock." Not "The Baptizer." Not "The Twin." He is forever "The Betrayer." Never mind that all the others fell away too. Judas is the Betrayer. There will be no Witness Protection for him either. Everyone knows who he is and will hate him forever for it.

You might know that the gospels were written at different times. Mark is the oldest, followed by Matthew and Luke. The youngest gospel is John. And you will notice that with each gospel, Judas looks progressively worse. As the church has more time to think and reflect on what happened, Judas gets worse coverage. In Mark, his actions are told as a matter of fact. By the time the Gospel of John rolls around, Judas is stealing money from the common purse and given names like the "Son of Perdition." And the hate on Judas didn't stop with the gospels. For centuries we have railed on him. Listen to these words from Papias, a second century bishop in Asia Minor.

"Judas was a dreadful, walking example of impiety in this world, with his flesh bloated to such an extent that he could not walk through a space where a wagon could easily pass. and his eyelids were so swollen that it was absolutely impossible for him to see the light and his eyes could not be seen by physicians, even with the help of a magnifying glass, so far had they sunk from their outward projection."[24]

Wow. That is just mean. I suppose there was no stopping the hate on him. He betrayed Jesus, for goodness sake, the one who claimed him, loved him and prayed for him. The one who washed his feet!

Not every Christian, though, was a hateful as Papias of Asia Minor. Not that they liked him, but for many Christians the focus has been on figuring him out, on wondering why. "Why would he do such a thing?" It is not unlike how we respond after each mass shooting. We want to know why. We quickly want to see what the shooter looks like. We want to line up our political arguments. We then want to figure out his problems. "Was he bullied? Was he active on social media? Did his parents abuse him? Did he have a mental history? Did he play lots of video games?" Once we get the data, we can categorize it. The shooting in Texas Church was a domestic violence thing. "Oh, ok." The kid in Colorado was bullied. "Oh, ok." Not that it makes it better, of course. It just sadly gives us some framework for thinking about the tragedy. We get none of that with Judas. We have no idea why he would betray Jesus. No reasons are given. The chief priests offer him thirty pieces of silver, but, at least in Mark's Gospel, he never asked for it.

For generations Christians have sought reasons. Maybe he thought Jesus was getting too extreme or not extreme enough. Maybe he thought Jesus was too big for his britches or not big enough. It is all speculation. Some so-called scholars have even sought to studying those famous Renaissance paintings of the betrayal, seeing if they can figure Judas' motives from those pictures... which were painted over 1000 years after the event happened! This is the coldest of cold cases. As disturbing as it may be, we will never figure out Judas. So we will just keep on hating that nasty, bloated, bug-eyed, Son of Perdition. Plus, he keeps us from looking at ourselves. [25]

Of course, what we know is that each one of us carries in us the possibility of such betrayal. All of us could have been him. Especially,

---

[24] Joan Acocella, "Betrayal," The New Yorker, August 3, 2009.
[25] ibid.

most especially, if we are prone to love Jesus. In fact, the frightening truth is that the more you follow, the more you give yourself to Christ, the more you love Christ, the greater the chance you will betray Christ! The very concept of betrayal requires that there is something to betray. Unless one has been personally involved in a relationship of trust, love and commitment, betrayal cannot occur. Unlike other sins, betrayal uses love to destroy what is love. That's why Judas kissed him. It is the sin of love against love. That is what is so painfully terrible about it. So, the closer one gets in love, the deeper the potential wound.

For the rest of the Roman world, Judas was just a finger-pointer. For the church, he is the worst. He betrayed. Therefore, he exposes to us the truth about us! He demonstrates the real danger in following Jesus. We could deeply wound him! *We* could be the betrayer! You recall that when Jesus said that those around the table would betray him, all the disciples began to ask, "Is it I?" They asked because they knew, somewhere deep inside, that it could be! It could have been any of them. It could have been any of us! We know betrayal. If we have loved, we do. We have been betrayed. And likely worse, we have done the betraying!

I suppose, it is probably time to stop condemning Judas. Because as bad as it was, his sin really didn't cause Jesus to die on that cross. "No human sin, not even betrayal, caused Jesus to die on that cross," says Gloria Johnson, "not the sins of the Pharisees, who delivered him over to Pilate, not the sins of Pilate, who delivered him over to the soldiers, not the sins of the soldiers, who nailed him to the cross. And therefore not the sin of Judas, who was his betrayer."[26] To say that human sin caused Jesus to die on the cross is to make Jesus the helpless victim rather than obedient servant. To say this empties the life of obedience of Jesus of any saving significance. Over and over during his three years of ministry, Jesus emphasized the point that he did not come to be served, but to serve, and to give his life for a ransom for others. Jesus had taken up his cross long before the notion of betrayal had entered the mind of Judas. As terrible as betrayal is, it would be even worse to see it as the cause of his death for it would take away from

---

[26] Rev. Gloria Johnson, White Memorial Presbyterian, Raleigh, NC, sermon, 1991.

Jesus his own motivation and source of meaning for that seminal event.

Jesus knew what he was getting into. Says one scholar, "Jesus knew before he came into the world that human love bears with it the seeds of betrayal. He wasn't surprised at the Last Supper when the disciples ask, 'Is it I?' Because he knew the sad capacity of the human heart, he did not regard Judas as someone to single out for rejection."[27] Throughout his ministry, Jesus showed love and tenderness to Judas. He prayed for him. He cared for him. He shared communion with him. He washed his feet even! Christ knows that our love is fragile, and it carries seeds of betrayal. Yet, he loves us all the same. We flee him as he approaches the cross. He approaches the cross, carrying our humanity with him because he loves us so. Ultimately, Christ's love of betrayers is stronger than the betrayers betraying.

When it comes to the death of Jesus, we are quick to place blame and slow to share it. We are even slower to understand that *that* very nature to "quickly place blame and avoid the share" is itself the reason Jesus' chooses to go to the cross. Everybody on the planet has the potential to betray. If you love someone, you can do them in. And that includes Jesus.

If you look back, there are actually two stories that wrap themselves around the Last Supper. One, of course, is sad Judas and his giving up Jesus. The other, though, is of a woman who gave *to* him. Listen to Mark 14:3-9. There are obvious differences in their stories, but what truly makes the difference is that the woman gives herself to the loss. Unlike Judas, she didn't manipulate the moment for personal gain. Unlike Judas, she didn't take any money. Unlike Judas, she wasn't deceptive or out to save her own skin. She doesn't seek to avoid the circumstances or profit from them. She doesn't deny the moment or herself. She doesn't say too much. She doesn't deny that she too could betray him. She doesn't make any foolish promises. She says nothing. She just acts. She acts in concert with the situation. She grieves for him. She shares in the Passion.

---

[27] Johnson.

I guess the truth is that we have the capacity for both these reactions - to bless him or bury him. Pray that we approach Lent with such awareness, that we not cast blame, that we do not declare righteousness, that we do not make wild judgments. But that we share in it, share in The Passion, that we may witness it once again and to allow it to save.

Thanks be to God.

Gone to Court
Mark 14:53-65

They took Jesus to the high priest; and all the chief priests, the elders, and the scribes were assembled. [54] Peter had followed him at a distance, right into the courtyard of the high priest; and he was sitting with the guards, warming himself at the fire. [55] Now the chief priests and the whole council were looking for testimony against Jesus to put him to death; but they found none. [56] For many gave false testimony against him, and their testimony did not agree. [57] Some stood up and gave false testimony against him, saying, [58] "We heard him say, 'I will destroy this temple that is made with hands, and in three days I will build another, not made with hands.'" [59] But even on this point their testimony did not agree. [60] Then the high priest stood up before them and asked Jesus, "Have you no answer? What is it that they testify against you?" [61] But he was silent and did not answer. Again the high priest asked him, "Are you the Messiah, the Son of the Blessed One?" [62] Jesus said, "I am; and 'you will see the Son of Man seated at the right hand of the Power,' and 'coming with the clouds of heaven.'" [63] Then the high priest tore his clothes and said, "Why do we still need witnesses? [64] You have heard his blasphemy! What is your decision?" All of them condemned him as deserving death. [65] Some began to spit on him, to blindfold him, and to strike him, saying to him, "Prophesy!" The guards also took him over and beat him.

Have you heard of the Innocence Project? It is a non-profit legal organization that works to free wrongfully convicted persons with the use of DNA evidence. Some of you might remember the case of Ronald Cotton, an Alamance County man convicted of the assault of a Burlington woman in 1985.[28] The victim identified her assailant in a police line-up. There was other evidence. A flashlight in his home resembled the one used by the assailant. Rubber from his tennis shoe was consistent with rubber found at the crime scene. He was sentenced to life in prison. Several appeals went nowhere. In 1994, a new defense emerged, with the help of DNA. After some tests, it was proven that

---

[28] Innocence Project. Ronald Cotton.
https://www.innocenceproject.org/cases/ronald-cotton/. Also National Registry of Exonerations. Ronald Cotton.
https://www.law.umich.edu/special/exoneration/Pages/casedetail.aspx?caseid=31 24

Cotton was not the assailant. Instead the guilty party was a man a few cell doors down. It was a groundbreaking event, if also shocking. Everyone was so sure Cotton was the man. Everyone was wrong. It is a shame the Innocent Project wasn't around some 2000 years ago because Jesus could've used it.

To pick up where we left off last week, Jesus has been arrested. One of his closest friends turned him over to the religious authorities who were after him. For some time the Jewish leadership saw Jesus as stepping out of line, so far out of line they had to do something. They wanted to arrest him, to get him out of the public arena. Judas solved that problem. Now they had Jesus in custody and could start their religious hearings against him.

One needs to understand that religious life was different. Religion wasn't just something you did on Sabbath Day. Temple wasn't just something you went to once a week. No, religion permeated Jewish life. People lived under the authority of the Torah and under the priests who studied that Torah. Laws were enforced, including religious law. If you stepped out of line with that law, there were consequences. This whole trial was about consequences.

If you ever wondered about the integrity of the due process around Jesus' trial, you need not look any further than the first line. "The chief priests and the whole council were looking for testimony against Jesus to put him to death, but they found none." You might think that since "they found none," that would be it. The hearing would be over. No, they kept going. They found no testimony that merited conviction, *but* they went ahead with the trial anyway. They were looking to arrest him since chapter three, by the way, and still didn't have anything. If this were a grand jury, there would be no reason to go forward. They proceed anyway. What then follows is a king kangaroo of the kangaroo courts.

There was a protocol for this type of crime. There was a due process. Sadly, it has been pointed out that some curious discrepancies occur in this trail of the century.[29] Capital trials were to take place only in the daytime. This one is at night. No legal procedures were to take place on a Sabbath Day. This one does. A death sentence could not be pronounced the same day as the trial. This one is. Trials were to be held in the official council chamber. This one meets in the home of the high priest. Prior examination of witnesses was required. That never happens. Curiously, all kinds of procedures are conveniently side-stepped or just plain ignored. For their own sake, the prosecution probably should have examined the witnesses, at the very least to get their stories straight. As it is, these two witnesses saw and heard two different things. None of that, though, seems to matter. Jesus is convicted, guilty before proven guilty.

The heart of the conviction is a report that Jesus said he would "destroy the temple and in three days build another." Just as religion wasn't simply religion back then, the temple wasn't simply a temple. Temple was the center of their faith. To talk ill of the temple was to talk ill of the faith, to speak ill of God himself. It wouldn't be tolerated. Curiously, there is no record of Jesus saying these words. In the Gospel of John, Jesus says "You destroy this temple and in three days I will raise it back up." That piece of clarifying information is never admitted into evidence.

Finally, the high priest puts Jesus on the stand, prodding him to hopefully say something to tilt the hearing in favor of the prosecution. "So, are *you* the messiah? The Son of the Blessed One?" he asks, half teasing him. Then, out of the blue, breaking his silence, Jesus suddenly turns state's evidence. "I AM." Just like that. You might say this is the center of Mark's Gospel. People have been asking that question for chapter upon chapter. Are you the messiah? Until now, Jesus has been coy or letting people try to answer for themselves. Suddenly, there is no hiding, there is no deception. There are no games. A direct question and an honest answer. "I AM. And you will see the Son of Man, seated at the right hand of the Power, coming with cloud of heaven."

---

[29] This section is assisted by notes from a Sunday School lesson by Richard L "Red" Jones, Alabama Supreme Court Judge, who often taught on this subject.

It is an admission of monumental proportions, confessing power, authority and eschatological purpose. "That's it!" They all point and shake. "We don't need any more witnesses! He has confessed!" Jesus even used language only reserved for God. Way back at the burning bush of Moses, God identified himself in that very way. "Who are you?" "I am who I am. I am who I will be." This is the language Jesus uses! They heard enough. They heard blasphemy. The hearing is over. The high priest looks like Perry Mason, and Jesus is taken away.

Often in cases tackled by the Innocence Project, two factors are in play. Either there is prosecutorial misconduct like in the Duke lacrosse case a few years ago or there is just plan blindness.[30] Here you have both. While there is definite misconduct, there is a whole lot of just plain ineptitude. All these people - these church people - leading this charge are blind to something. They are missing it. Think about it. The Scribes and Pharisees are congratulating themselves. They see a guilty man being rightfully convicted by good evidence and an ingenious prosecution. The Scribes and Pharisees seem to see it all playing out one way. But in fact, there is a larger story that indicates that something else is playing out on a far deeper level.

Consider all this talk about the temple. They are worried about their precious temple. Yet, when you think of Jesus saying these words, you start thinking that maybe Jesus wasn't talking about the same thing they were. Jesus seems to be talking something besides brick and mortar. Jesus seems to be talking about another kind of temple and referring to another kind of destroying and indicating another kind of rebuilding. It begs the question, "what is the temple?" More specifically, it begs the question, "what is *your* temple?" What is it that you have put all your heart in, all your chips in? What is it that you will defend to death, that for which you will kill? What is your temple? What blinds you to seeing and knowing Christ more fully, more clearly?

Some people think Jesus made a tactical mistake saying anything that could be interpreted as bad-mouthing the temple. They say he could

---

[30] Innocent Project. Duke Lacrosse. https://www.innocenceproject.org/the-legacy-of-the-duke-case/

have done all this without disparaging the sacred store. You don't pull on Superman's cape, as they say.[31]   I imagine, though, that is exactly what Jesus' intended to do. It is what Jesus always intends to do. Jesus went to the heart of their glory and said their heart was in the wrong place. There is nothing wrong with the temple, per se. Jesus went there himself, many times. There is nothing wrong with temple, up until it seduces you away from the truth.

You can't get out of Mark 14 without asking the question, "what is your temple?" Is it a past you can't get over? Is it a future you can't stop wishing for? Is it a crutch you can't drop? In most cases it is more than even that, though. In most cases, the temple is the person you *think* you are. You think you are a person who doesn't follow that close to Jesus. Or you think you are a person who already knows what you think and believe. Or you think you are a person who doesn't like to be fooled. Or you think you are a person who doesn't like organized religion. Or you think you are a person who really, really likes organized religion a whole lot! Or you think you are a person who likes law and order. Or you think you are a person who likes social justice. And that very certitude of self makes you highly unlikely to be open to anything new that Christ might be doing. You only see the Christ you want to see, expect to see. And any messiah who appears that doesn't match it, you will slaughter.

Trials are about choosing. Jesus knows that. Whatever we value most, Christ will at some point make us chose. We will have to choose between Christ and whatever institution, whatever project, whatever achievement, whatever ideological construct, whatever political position, or whatever sociological experiment upon which we have set our identity.

Donald Miller tells the story of his coming to terms with faith. He spent his life fighting for social change and social justice. Then he came to a crisis.[32]

---

[31] Jim Croce, "Don't Mess Around with Jim," <u>Don't Mess Around with Jim</u>. New York: ABC Records, 1971.
[32] Donald Miller. <u>Blue Like Jazz</u>. (Nashville: Thomas Nelson Press, 2003).

"I think every conscious person, every person who is awake to the functioning principles within his reality, has a moment where he stops blaming the problems in the world on group think, on humanity and authority, and start to face... himself. I hate this more than anything. This is the hardest principle within Christian spirituality for me to deal with. The problem is not out there. The problem is the needy beat of a thing that lives in my chest."

"Do I want social justice for the oppressed or do I just want to be known as a person who wants social justice for the oppressed. I spend 95 percent of my time thinking about myself anyway. I don't have to watch the evening news to see the world is bad, I only have to look at myself. I am not just browbeating myself here. I am only saying that true change, true life-giving, God-honoring change would have to start with the individual. I was the very problem I had been protesting. I wanted to make a new sign: 'I AM THE PROBLEM.'"

There is a reason Jesus goes after their precious temple. Because our religious certitudes must be taken down before we share in the temple that Christ is working out in us and around us.

You know what might be most disturbing? These religious leaders have been looking for their messiah for generations. Their Holy Scriptures have been pointing to this Chosen One since the time of King David. They have studied, discussed, debated and prayed about this moment for years. Then, finally, one arrives and announces that he is, in fact, that messiah. Now granted, anyone would understand a level of suspicion or at least a desire to check it out carefully. Their response, though, is denial .... and not just denial, but violence!

Their entire hope has been based on a messiah. Yet when one arrives identifying himself as such, they beat him, and have him killed. That isn't just mean, it is bizarre. They destroyed the very thing they sought. They did all this because of a religious certitude, because of their precious temple. You would think they would be the very ones to recognize the messiah or at least the first to want a fair and thoughtful hearing! Not so. They end up being the first ones to beat him. Clearly, they decided, early on, that Jesus was a threat. They predetermined he was a threat, a threat to the things they valued most, to the most religious things in their life. It is ironic, but it is true.

Our religious certitudes must be dismantled for those are the very threats to Christ. They prevent us from being open to the new precisely because they are built on what we want and think. Our religious certitudes must be dismantled for they are threats to Christ being able to build anything new in our hearts. These are not easy Scriptures to read. These are not pleasant, Sunday morning topics. No one comes out looking good in these reports. No one is innocent. Well, one is. And the closer He gets to Good Friday, the more we realize how much we need Him there.

Thanks be to God.

Went After What?

John 12:9-19

The next day the great crowd that had come to the festival heard that Jesus was coming to Jerusalem. ¹³ So they took branches of palm trees and went out to meet him, shouting, "Hosanna! Blessed is the one who comes in the name of the Lord— the King of Israel!" ¹⁴ Jesus found a young donkey and sat on it; as it is written: ^{15"Do} not be afraid, daughter of Zion. Look, your king is coming, sitting on a donkey's colt!" ¹⁶ His disciples did not understand these things at first; but when Jesus was glorified, then they remembered that these things had been written of him and had been done to him. ¹⁷ So the crowd that had been with him when he called Lazarus out of the tomb and raised him from the dead continued to testify. ¹⁸ It was also because they heard that he had performed this sign that the crowd went to meet him. ¹⁹ The Pharisees then said to one another, "You see, you can do nothing. Look, the world has gone after him!"

What a difference a word makes. Or even a few words. "The Pharisees said to one another, "See, you can't do anything. Look, the world has gone after him." These Pharisees have been trying to bring him down for a while. They have not liked his preaching, his healing, his caring. They have not liked it because he goes against their grain, because is speaking blasphemy. They find him to be a troublemaker. So they have been looking for a way to get him, but they can't get him because, to their disgust, he has become too popular. He has become too much of a thing. He has become a hit.

You see this often. A few years ago LSU wanted to fire its football coach. The administration at the university decided Coach Les Miles was ineffective. They were not winning as much as they thought they should. They didn't like the way he bumped up against authority. His record had slipped, so it was as good of a time as any. Then Miles notched some unexpected wins. The players lifted him up on their shoulders. He made a teary address. The crowds chanted his name, and the administration backed off. They couldn't do anything. He was too big, too popular. The college football world had gone after him. Crowds can be like that.

Every gospel shares the story of the triumphal entry into Jerusalem. Every gospel talks about the donkey ride, the garments spread along the road and the hosannas cascading upon him as he enters the city. None of the gospels, though, go into the drama of the crowd as much as John. The great crowds, as John calls them, are enthusiastic and overwhelming. They are the story within the story.

Word spread quickly about Jesus raising a dead man. Of course it would. When word then got out that Jesus returned to Lazarus' house, that he was there having dinner, the whole town showed up. Look at verse 9. "When the great crowd learned that he was there, they came not only because of Jesus but also to see Lazarus, whom he raised from the dead." Scripture says the great crowd of people came not only "because of Jesus, but to see Lazarus." Suddenly and curiously, Jesus is a bit of an after-thought. "Yea, Jesus is nice, but where is Lazarus?!" Moreover, the verse doesn't say "meet" or "speak with" or "hear his testimony" or any number of more conversational words. No, they just want to "see" him. They want to see him, like you would a circus act. It sounds like one of those shows at the fair. "Come see the bearded lady! Come see the world's biggest alligator! Come see Lazarus!" Of course, it is a great crowd. Everyone likes a spectacle. Jesus and his act have become a spectacle. The world has gone after him.

The next day, the word spreads that Jesus is coming into the city. So again, a great crowd gathers. They rip branches from palm trees and run out of the city gate to greet him, to wave him in, like they would a conquering king, like they would a prized fighter entering a ring for the big fight. The crowd gathers to see a show. The crowd gathers, not because they necessarily know him or because they want to know him, but because of the crazy things he does. Maybe he will juggle this time. Maybe he will pull a rabbit out of a hat. It is no wonder the Pharisees can't touch him. The world has gone after him.

That is an important line. "The world has gone after him." One might think it is a good thing. "Oh good. The world is going after him." Isn't that what we want? People to clamor around and for Jesus? But for some reason, we don't trust this crowd though, do we? And not simply because we know the rest of the story. For some reason, we get the sense that they are going after him for all the wrong reasons.

Often in these gospels, whenever Jesus does a miracle, he immediately tells those witnessing, "By the way, don't tell anyone you saw this." We often wonder, why not? For Jesus, though, being Jesus is never about putting on a show, but pointing to a greater purpose. Jesus never was interested in starting a circus but establishing a community that sought to live and serve under the Kingdom of God. By the time he gets to Jerusalem though, it seems too late. The world's gone after him. Public opinion and first century social media have spoken. They have themselves a circus. However, if we know anything about the world, we know the world is fickle. It will change on a dime. Six months after Les Miles saved his job, crowds of fanatical Bayou Bengal fans were marching in the streets, demanding they fire the man. So it will be of course with Jesus. They will turn and demand he be crucified.

The Gospel of John tells the story of Jesus' entry into Jerusalem and his preparation for the cross. Through it all, the gospel provides lessons for those willing to learn. Certainly there is a lesson in these foolish crowds. We too can become nothing more than band-wagon fans of Christ, cheering loud when there is something to cheer about and cursing his name when things turn sour. There is also a lesson, though, in theses disciples. You'll notice that through all of this chaos, the disciples are rather cautious. At least in the Gospel of John they are. Crowds are cheering and clamoring, and the disciples seem dumbstruck. It is a little unsettling. All these people are so very excited and wound up about Jesus, but those who have been following him most closely seem confused, anxious and hesitant. Shouldn't it be the other way around? But that is not how it is in this gospel. There is a lot of excitement and noise, just not from the disciples. They clearly didn't understand what was happening. That is what the scripture says. They didn't understand these things. They would, later. Later they would, after he was glorified, after he died on the cross and was raised from the dead. It just would take them some time.

The last few weeks, we have talked a lot about the disciples. We have talked about how they failed Jesus, how they betrayed him, left him and fled from him, in this time of crisis, in this time of need. Each one of them. Peter. Judas, to name the obvious ones, but they all did. They were a sad bunch. But it is worth noting at least this much. At least they made the effort! What the Gospel of John witnesses to so beautifully is that these rag-tag disciples are a confused, thick-headed, wrong-minded, miss-stepping, and constantly failing bunch. Yet, given some time and the work of the Holy Spirit, they too can figure out a few things out. Moreover, they can even be witnesses. Peter ends up being the rock the church is founded upon. That is an irony of all ironies. The one who couldn't admit to knowing Jesus soon becomes his most vocal witness.

I guess the lesson is that discipleship of Jesus is not a parade. It is not a football game or a basketball tournament where you pick the winner and ride your bracket with enthusiasm and confidence. Quite the contrary, discipleship of Jesus is a long race. It is a cross country meet, full of up and downs, twist and turns, getting lost and having to recalculate. Some things you don't figure out until late in the game. Some things you never figure out! It is a long race.

The same world that has "gone after" Jesus, will soon "go after" him for the purpose of killing him. And we have a hand in that too, of course. But discipleship is not about the whims of emotions, the ride of cultural sentiment or even the temperature of our heart. Discipleship is about following. Discipleship is about following...even if at a distance. The Gospel of Mark says that Peter "followed at a distance." That is not great, not evidence of great confidence, but at least he is still following!

Yes, discipleship is about love. The gospel calls us to love the Lord our God with our heart, soul and mind. That is not to say that we are always emotional about it. It is not to say we are to love as a star-struck pre-teen. It means we are to love as an abiding friend. It means we love with depth and explore that depth.

Yes, discipleship is about faith. That is not to say, though, that faith is always certain about things. Years ago, Anselm of Canterbury, an early church theologian, advocated that Christian life is faith seeking understanding. One doesn't figure it all, understand it all and then get faith. No, one begins in faith and then seeks to understand.

Yes, discipleship is about victory. But it is a victory found first in loss. "The cross is laid on every Christian. The first Christ-suffering which every man must experience is the call to abandon the attachments of this world. It is that dying of the old man which is the result of his encounter with Christ. As we embark upon discipleship, we surrender ourselves to

Christ in union with his death—we give over our lives to death. Thus it begins; the cross is not the terrible end to an otherwise God-fearing and happy life, but it meets us at the beginning of our communion with Christ. When Christ calls a man, he bids him come and die."[33] Those are words from Dietrich Bonhoeffer. Now that will not appease a hungry crowd. That won't sell well. It isn't flashy. It takes some time to let that sink in. It takes some time to figure it out, to figure out what that means to you, to figure out what treasure awaits those who do. But one must die in order to live. Ask Lazarus.

If you want to know what "going after" Christ should look like, John will show you. You just back up a few verses. Back up a few verses to Mary and Martha. They aren't cheering. They are not gawking and shouting. They are silently washing his feet. They aren't looking for a circus. They are sharing in his suffering. They weep when we weep, so they might rejoice when he rejoices.

Peter may have put it best. Several days later, after all these events played out, after Jesus is glorified and after Peter begins to understand, he finally has something to proclaim. It is not superficial emotiveness. It clearly rises from something deeper. I have discovered, he says, that

"The Lord is always before me. He is my right hand. So that I am not ever shaken. My heart is glad. My tongue rejoices. My flesh lives in hope. I will not be abandoned. I have come to know the ways of life and God makes me full of gladness with his presence."

That is a hallelujah that sticks. One the world should go after.

Thanks be to God.

---

[33] Dietrich Bonhoeffer. The Cost of Discipleship. (New York: MacMillan Publishing, 1937).

The Folly of the Cross
Matthew 28:1-10, I Corinthians 1: 18-31

After the sabbath, as the first day of the week was dawning, Mary Magdalene and the other Mary went to see the tomb. ²And suddenly there was a great earthquake; for an angel of the Lord, descending from heaven, came and rolled back the stone and sat on it. ³His appearance was like lightning, and his clothing white as snow. ⁴For fear of him the guards shook and became like dead men. ⁵But the angel said to the women, "Do not be afraid; I know that you are looking for Jesus who was crucified. ⁶He is not here; for he has been raised, as he said. Come, see the place where he lay. ⁷Then go quickly and tell his disciples, 'He has been raised from the dead, and indeed he is going ahead of you to Galilee; there you will see him.' This is my message for you." ⁸So they left the tomb quickly with fear and great joy and ran to tell his disciples. ⁹Suddenly Jesus met them and said, "Greetings!" And they came to him, took hold of his feet, and worshiped him. ¹⁰Then Jesus said to them, "Do not be afraid; go and tell my brothers to go to Galilee; there they will see me."

For the message about the cross is foolishness to those who are perishing, but to us who are being saved it is the power of God. ¹⁹For it is written,

"I will destroy the wisdom of the wise,
  and the discernment of the discerning I will thwart."

²⁰Where is the one who is wise? Where is the scribe? Where is the debater of this age? Has not God made foolish the wisdom of the world? ²¹For since, in the wisdom of God, the world did not know God through wisdom, God decided, through the foolishness of our proclamation, to save those who believe. ²²For Jews demand signs and Greeks desire wisdom, ²³but we proclaim Christ crucified, a stumbling block to Jews and foolishness to Gentiles, ²⁴but to those who are the called, both Jews and Greeks, Christ the power of God and the wisdom of God. ²⁵For God's foolishness is wiser than human wisdom, and God's weakness is stronger than human strength.

Today is April Fool's Day. When I was a child, my grandfather would call my sister and me on April Fool's Day to fool us with some wild tale. "Your grandmother and I just adopted a snake!" It is supposed to snow 12 inches tomorrow!" "Oh my! An elephant got loose from the zoo and is running down your street!" We would run to the window and look. Alas, no elephant. "April Fools!" And he would laugh and laugh. He would make these calls for years. Eventually, we figured it out, but that didn't stop the calls. Every year, the same thing. So, we would humor him. "An elephant? Oh no. I'll go look out the window. Oh gosh, no elephant. You got me again Granddad." And, still, he would laugh and laugh. Fast forward a few years. My father employed the same technique on my children. "Your grandmother and I just adopted a snake!' "It is supposed to snow 12 inches tomorrow." One year, my father tried the elephant prank. "Hey Jack! An elephant got loose from the zoo and is running down your street!" My son, though, is different. Jack did not think it was funny. He was all of five, and it only freaked him out. When he heard about the elephant, he dropped his toys, ran inside, locked the doors and hid under his bed. Some jokes don't work like you thought they would.

Here on this April Fool's Day, there is nothing funny going on in the Gospel of Matthew. As a matter of fact, Matthew might be the cruelest account of the crucifixion. The mocking seems worse in Matthew. The conspiracies seem more elaborate. Jesus gets no sympathy from the other executed criminals. No women weep for him in Matthew. Even God seems to abandon him. It certainly is the most violent of the Gospels. Heck, an earthquake shakes the whole scene. Death doesn't bring any dignity and relief either. A squadron of guards is posted at his tomb. No one is laughing in this story.

The most curious thing to me in, though, is all the work these people go through to keep Jesus dead. Pharisees, chief priests and Roman leaders have conspired to kill him. Now, after he is dead, they gather again to figure out what to do next. "We need to keep this tomb secure. Otherwise someone will steal his body and pretend he didn't die." They say this even though the disciples have scattered like frightened sheep and are certainly even more scattered after seeing the way Rome deals with people like Jesus!

The Pharisees remembered what Jesus' said about being alive in three days. (Funny, the disciples didn't seem to remember it, but the Pharisees did.) So they want a guard posted. They want the tomb secure. They put a guard on the tomb of a dead man so he can't leave. Sounds just like the government, doesn't it? But they are not finished.

They want to spread rumors about the disciples too. So they pay-off some soldiers to tell stories about the disciples.

Is it me or are these people going to a whole lot of work trying to keep a dead man dead? They use every powerful tool at their disposal - religious authority, military might, legal influence, governmental weight, social contacts, financial assets. They use every resource they have. They desperately want him to stay dead, don't they? You might even say it is a little comical - doing all these things to keep a dead man dead. You could say it is all a little foolish. But don't say that! Because we are the foolish ones. That is what the world will tell you.

There are so many things about Christianity that allow for an easy accommodation in and with culture. There are so many elements of faith that make for a harmonious life. Christianity gives one a moral framework within which to live and raise your children. It gives one a sense of peace and ease about one's death and life after death. It provides one a purpose to work for the common good, which benefits communities. It calls individuals to be good stewards of the earth, to care for the less fortunate, to treat others fairly, to be honest and faithful. Faithful Christians make good neighbors. But there is one thing that is awkward. There is one thing is forever going to be a sticking point in this world. There is one thing that will make you stick out like a sore thumb. There is one thing that you cannot get around. There is a foolishness to faith. There is a foolishness to faith in the resurrection. You know it. I know it. Everyone knows it. This isn't just a modernity matter. It was as odd then, as it is now. You can say you believe God created the world. You can say you believe in a Holy Spirit. You can even affirm a life after death. That is all fine. Many people would get around those beliefs. But when you say you believe in the resurrection of Jesus...well... that is a stumbling block.

We like to laugh at some of the bizarre things we hear in the Quran-an. We all like to roll our eyes at the many lives in Hindu faith. And nothing draws a response like the Tom Cruise religion - What is it? Scientology? Founded by L. Ron Hubbard? He sounds like a vacuum cleaner salesman. Just mentioning that gets a laugh. But we better be careful, because for every strange story in some other religion, we have Jesus raising from the dead. It is foolishness to the world. It is. It is foolishness to the world and those who call themselves Christians are marked with it, whether we like it or not. It marks us. To the world it is foolishness.

But I believe it. I do. I believe it. I can't prove it. I can't explain it. Yet I know it and experience it. And if you search your heart, you might too because it is not about what you know, but what you trust, what you trust about the God of Scripture. Evidence and proofs will never get you to belief. William Placher says "It is only when our hearts and minds have been captured by the Jesus we meet in the scriptures or in the church or out on the road."[34] That is where they began to understand and trust a resurrected Jesus - when he met them on the road.

Do you recall what the disciples did when they experienced the resurrected Lord? They worshiped him. They worshiped him, not simply because he was alive. They saw that in Lazarus. They worshiped him, not just because it was a grand show. They worshiped him because they figured out that he was who he said he was, because he did what he said he would do. The Messiah was indeed a Messiah, and the Messiah was true to his word. They had experienced and recognized the work of the living Lord in their life and in the world. That compelled them to worship. Foolishness be damned.

The world says it is foolish to believe that. Really? Well then what is foolish? I guess I am a little confused on the world's definition of foolishness. We produce more food in this world than ever before and yet hunger affects some 700 million people across the globe. That is not foolish? A third our food gets thrown away and a 7th of our population is hungry. That is not foolish? We have more ways to get water than ever before, and yet 780 million don't have ready access to clean water.[35] That is not foolish? Each decade, the number of mass shootings rise, including those at schools. Since Sandy Hook, we have had about 200 school shootings, but we can't find a thoughtful, meaning way to address the issue outside of our usual politicized

[34] William C. Placher. Jesus the Savior: The Meaning of Jesus Christ for Christian Faith. (Louisville: WJKP, 2001).
[35] Mary Thomas Watkins. Water: The Cycle of Life. Address at North Carolina Soil and Water Conservation Function. Raleigh, May 2018.

talking points. That is not foolish? We have less and less people coming to church, and congregations want to argue about this carpet color? We have less and less people becoming Christian, and we want to worry if the ones coming in the door are white or black, rich or poor, gay or straight? That is not foolish?

There is a lot of things we just take as normal that seem foolish to me. So what is foolish? To believe in something gracious. To believe that God so loved the world that God gave God's only son? To believe that God is love and those who abide in love about in God? That is foolish compared to the other stuff we hear and see? I guess between the world's definition of foolishness and God's, I'll take God's.

You know what I always have thought was funny? I have always that it was funny that when it comes to belief, the crucifixion is never doubted. The resurrection is, but the crucifixion is not. Think about that. No one really doubts that Jesus was likely crucified - that the religious authorities instigated it, that the Roman leadership agreed to it, and that all his friends abandoned him to it. We don't doubt that, do we? We don't doubt that because we know that kind of thing can happen in the kind of world, we live in. That makes sense with our experience of the world. What does that say about us?! What does that say about this world? What does it say about this world that has such very clear ideas about foolishness?

So, go ahead, call me a fool. It is not a terrible thing to be a fool, by the way. It is not a terrible label. Some of you, back in college or high school, had to read *King Lear*.[36] *King Lear* is one of William Shakespeare's grand plays. An aging British king decides to step down from the throne and divide his kingdom among his three daughters. Arrogant, self-possessed, he demands they all shower him with praise to determine who will get what. The two oldest daughters fall over themselves in syrupy praise. The youngest, Cordelia, says she really doesn't have words to describe her feelings. The King doesn't like this answer and demands something better. She, though, refuses to lie about her emotions. She loves him, what can she say? "I cannot heave

---

[36] William Shakespeare, <u>King Lear</u> (Oxford: Clarendon Press, 1877).

my heart into my mouth. I love thee according to our bond. No more. No less."

Well, that will not do. Lear banishes her to France without a dowry. For good measure, he bans a lot of the others too. The only one left to follow him is the fool, who constantly tries to talk sense into the king. Lear, of course, dismisses the fool. "What would the fool ever know?" Well, before you know it, the great king is exiled in his own land, wandering the heath among the violent storm, seeking refuge from his tormentors' cruel schemes. At the height of the storm, stuck in driving rain, without kingdom, without a home shivers a broken king. He has disowned his only good child. He is tormented by two cruel ones. He gets advice from fools. He is no longer robed in fine apparel. He is neither marked with the badges of valor and honor. He is left soaked to his bones. At this point, to find at least some relief from the storm, the fool finds a cave and calls the king, "Enter here, my lord!" After raging against the chaos for a while, the king relents. The king then speaks his first sensible words in pages. "No, in boy, go first. You get thee in. I'll pray."

It is a small line in a big play, but it is pivotal. For the first time the king gives way to someone else. "In boy, you go first." For the first time, the king humbles himself for the sake of another. For the first time, the king follows the fool. For the first time, the king prays.

> *"Poor naked wretches, wheresoe'er you are,*
> *that bide the pelting of this pitiless storm,*
> *how shall your houseless heads and unfed sides,*
> *your looped and windowed raggedness*
> *defend you from seasons such as these?*
> *O, I have ta'en too little care of this!*
> *Take physic, pomp, expose thyself to feel what wretches feel,*
> *that thou mayst shake the superflux to them,*
> *and show the heavens more just."*

I know King Lear isn't a religious story, but there is something faithful here. For the first time, the king prays. The king humbles himself for the sake of another. The king follows the fool, ironically, the only one who makes sense in the whole play. Oh, that we would follow the fool from Nazareth, who said all kinds of foolish things, things that got him killed. Oh, that we would follow the fool who is the Son of God.

There is a foolishness to being a Christian, and Easter comes around once a year just to remind us of it, in case we were getting too comfortable. Easter comes around so that we don't get confused, so we don't begin to think the foolishness of the world is normal. Easter is woven in creation to remind us that death does not have the last say - or hate or terror or hurt or evil or sin or suffering or things present or things to come. It is true then. It is true now.

And, perhaps, no one puts it better than Paul.

"For the message about the cross is foolishness to those who are perishing, but to us who are being saved it is the power of God. For it is written, "I will destroy the wisdom of the wise, and the discernment of the discerning I will thwart." Where is the one who is wise? Where is the scribe? Where is the debater of this age? Has not God made foolish the wisdom of the world? For since, in the wisdom of God, the world did not know God through wisdom, God decided, through the foolishness of our proclamation, to save those who believe. For Jews demand signs and Greeks desire wisdom, but we proclaim Christ crucified, a stumbling block to Jews and foolishness to Gentiles, but to those who are the called, both Jews and Greeks, Christ the power of God and the wisdom of God. For God's foolishness is wiser than human wisdom, and God's weakness is stronger than human strength. Consider your own call, brothers and sisters: not many of you were wise by human standards, not many were powerful, not many were of noble birth. But God chose what is foolish in the world to shame the wise; God chose what is weak in the world to shame the strong; God chose what is low and despised in the world, things that are not, to reduce to nothing things that are, so that no one might boast in the presence of God."

Today is Easter.

Happy April Fool's Day.

Thanks be to God.

Preaching Themes

Where You are From
John 6:41-51, Romans 8:10-17

Then the Jews began to complain about him because he said, "I am the bread that came down from heaven." 42 They were saying, "Is not this Jesus, the son of Joseph, whose father and mother we know? How can he now say, 'I have come down from heaven'?" 43 Jesus answered them, "Do not complain among yourselves. 44 No one can come to me unless drawn by the Father who sent me; and I will raise that person up on the last day. 45 It is written in the prophets, 'And they shall all be taught by God.' Everyone who has heard and learned from the Father comes to me. 46 Not that anyone has seen the Father except the one who is from God; he has seen the Father. 47 Very truly, I tell you, whoever believes has eternal life. 48 I am the bread of life. 49 Your ancestors ate the manna in the wilderness, and they died. 50 This is the bread that comes down from heaven, so that one may eat of it and not die. 51 I am the living bread that came down from heaven. Whoever eats of this bread will live forever; and the bread that I will give for the life of the world is my flesh."

But if Christ is in you, though the body is dead because of sin, the Spirit is life because of righteousness. 11 If the Spirit of him who raised Jesus from the dead dwells in you, he who raised Christ from the dead will give life to your mortal bodies also through his Spirit that dwells in you. 12 So then, brothers and sisters, we are debtors, not to the flesh, to live according to the flesh— 13 for if you live according to the flesh, you will die; but if by the Spirit you put to death the deeds of the body, you will live. 14 For all who are led by the Spirit of God are children of God. 15 For you did not receive a spirit of slavery to fall back into fear, but you have received a spirit of adoption. When we cry, "Abba! Father!" 16 it is that very Spirit bearing witness with our spirit that we are children of God, 17 and if children, then heirs, heirs of God and joint heirs with Christ—if, in fact, we suffer with him so that we may also be glorified with him.

Not long after I moved from Alabama to take an associate position at White Memorial Presbyterian in Raleigh, I was invited to a party. Some young folks from the church were having a cook-out. That evening I saw someone I knew, someone from my hometown, from my home church actually. I saw Chris. Except no one called him Chris. Everyone was calling him John, which was terribly confusing to me. I thought he was Chris. He looked like Chris. He sounded like Chris.

Apparently, he was John. I went up to him, "Hey, Chris!" He said, "No, I'm John. You can call me John."

Well, that was different. And Chris... John was different. From what I remembered, Chris was quiet and bookish. John was not like that at all. John was demonstrative and gregarious. Back in Birmingham, Chris was sometimes the object of teasing from the older boys. This John was different. He had a new confidence, a new job, and apparently a new identity. Yet I felt like I "had one" on John. I knew his secret. I knew John was actually Chris. "I know who you are," I thought. "You can't fool me! I know where you are from!"

This happens sometimes with folks, doesn't it? They want to leave home and change. They head off to college or join the service. They become something new. I remember seeing high school friends in college. They traded in their Member's Only jacket for Birkenstocks and flannel shirts. They took down their Flock of Seagulls style, grew out their hair and added a beard. They tried to be different, but you knew. You knew the truth. "I know who you are! You can't fool me! I know where you are from!"

It happens. It happens in Scripture, to Jesus of all people. It is one of the "come back down to earth" moments of the Bible. Jesus preaches, "I am the bread of life," and everyone says, "No, you're not. You're Joseph's son!" It is one of the repeated criticisms of Jesus. In fact, it is the one criticism he can't seem to get past. They knew where he was from. "I have come down from heaven, to do the will of him who sent me." "No, you don't come down from heaven. You come from Nazareth!" One needs to remember what was happening in ancient Israel at that time. Romans occupied the land. Gentiles were moving in, into places like Nazareth. Identities were threatened. Ties that bind were unbinding. These people were on edge. Their "home," their world was coming apart. "Where did this man get this wisdom and these deeds of power? Is not this the carpenter's son? Is not his mother called Mary? And are not his brothers James and Joseph and Simon and Judas? And are not all his sisters with us?" It is the same story. "We know who you are! You can't fool us! We know where you are from! "

Where you are from is important. Where you are from says a lot about you. Where you are from shapes you. It can shape how you talk, what you eat, who you like, what you believe, and in ways you hardly notice. It is true of the country of which you are a citizen, the region in which you live, of the state to which you pay taxes and the town from which you come. We carry those labels, often proudly and sometimes defensively. It is my country, my region, my state and my hometown. We often relish in them, celebrate them even - on the 4th of July across the country, during the weekend of the ACC tournament in North Carolina, or at the whirligig festival in Wilson.

Having something with which to identify is important.[37] It can stabilize a youngster growing up. It can ease anxiety of parents raising kids. It can give us a sense of constancy and security. "I belong here. They have to take me because I was born to them!" That is comforting. But we all know, and we have all seen the downside of "where are you from." It can create xenophobia - a fear of anything outside of where you're from. It can create a hodophobia - fear of traveling beyond where you're from. It can make one restrictive of who you let in. It can make one possessive of those who want out.

Thomas Wolfe penned his famous North Carolina novel in 1929. In many ways it was autobiographical, the story of Wolfe and his hometown of Asheville. The book, though, spoke too much truth and aired much of the town's dirty laundry. Now, Wolfe changed the names of people and of places to protect them, but a thoughtful reader could read between the lines. When he spoke of Altamonte, he meant Asheville; when he went to school in Pulpit Hill, he meant Chapel Hill; when he met a girl from Little Richmond, he meant Little Washington. It didn't take much for native Carolinians to figure it out. Apparently, people in Asheville quickly figured it out and made life pretty miserable for Wolfe. The prophet can never go home again![38]

Jesus didn't go back home. In fact, he never really made a home. Have you ever noticed that? Jesus moved out, but never again moved in anywhere else. Some might say he was an itinerant preacher. Others

---

[37] Erik Erikson, Identity: Youth and Crisis. (New York: Norton & Company, 1968).
[38] Thomas Wolfe, Look Homeward, Angel. (New York: Scribner's and Sons, 1929).

might say he was a gypsy. He said this, "Foxes have holes, and birds of the air have nests; but the Son of Man has nowhere to lay his head."

What did he mean by this? Well, it was a response to statement someone made to him. As they were walking down a road, someone said, "I will follow you wherever you go!" "Really?" Jesus replies. "Foxes have holes, and birds of the air have nests; but the Son of Man has nowhere to lay his head." This is more than a statement about how much walking they would be doing. This is a statement of identity, of home. Jesus was never bound to a place. No one place shaped him, molded him, made him. He may have been from Nazareth, but Jesus never settled in anywhere. He stayed on the road, moving from town to town, to village to village, from house to house. He didn't have a home. His home was with God. This isn't just a spiritualized answer. His home was with God. That is where he found security, identity and belonging. That was where he found welcome, purpose and direction. Having a home with God kept him free.

Everybody is going to ancestry. com.[39] Everyone wants to find out where they are from. "I am this. I am that. I am from here. I am from there." It seems very interesting, but I am not sure what it ultimately tells you. So you are 1/8 French. What do you do with that information? How much peace and purpose, security and identity do we get from it? And I guess if we go back far enough, we are all kind of related, right?

What we discover is that a home in God gives us a place that isn't bound by blood lines. God gives us a place that can't be bulldozed over for another Wal-Mart. It gives us a place that is not decided by which side of the track we were born, or where our daddy worked. It gives us a place that is not subject to human frailty or arbitrary rules of admission. Romans 8: "All who are led by the Spirit of God are children of God. You did not receive a spirit of slavery- abandonment. You have received a spirit of adoption - freedom. When we cry, "Father!" it is that very Spirit bearing witness with our Spirit that we

---

[39] Gregory Rodriguez. "Why Are Americans So Obsessed with Genealogy? http://www.whatitmeanstobeamerican.org/imperfect-union/why-are-americans-so-obsessed-with-genealogy/

are children of God, and if children of God, then heirs of God joint heirs with Christ."

There is a restlessness in this world. There was back then, and there is now. Whether you are trying to find a place to give you peace, keep a place that seems to be falling apart or leave a place that is failing you, no place is perfect. No people are pure. No home, town, region or country is "all that." That is what you hear in Thomas Wolf's book. Home can as much as a burden as a blessing. Despite where we are brought-up, there is but one redemptive place.

One of my favorite scriptures falls at the end of Revelation. It almost reads as a summary in my mind of the gospel, a "so it comes to this" kind of conclusion. It embraces a vision of the future that is about place, though not as we usually think. The Scripture is Rev 21.

> *I saw a new heaven and a new earth;*
> *for the first heaven and the first earth had passed away,*
> *and the sea was no more.*
> *And I saw the holy city, the new Jerusalem,*
> *coming down out of heaven from God,*
> *prepared as a bride adorned for her husband.*
> *And I heard a loud voice from the throne.*
> *And it said,*
> *See, the home of God is with people.*
> *God will be with his people;*
> *They will be God's people*
> *and God himself will be with them.*
> *And God will wipe every tear from their eyes.*
> *And Death will be no more;*
> *and mourning and crying and pain will be no more,*
> *for the first things have passed away."*

The home of God is with people. And our home is with God. St. Augustine: "Thou has made us for thyself, O Lord, and our heart is restless until it finds it rest in Thee."[40]

Thanks be to God.

---

[40] Augustine, of Hippo. The Confessions of Saint Augustine. (Mt Vernon: Peter Pauper Press, 1949).

What You Eat
John 6: 51-66, Romans 14: 17-20

I am the living bread that came down from heaven. Whoever eats of this bread will live forever; and the bread that I will give for the life of the world is my flesh."

52 The Jews then disputed among themselves, saying, "How can this man give us his flesh to eat?" 53 So Jesus said to them, "Very truly, I tell you, unless you eat the flesh of the Son of Man and drink his blood, you have no life in you. 54 Those who eat my flesh and drink my blood have eternal life, and I will raise them up on the last day; 55 for my flesh is true food and my blood is true drink. 56 Those who eat my flesh and drink my blood abide in me, and I in them. 57 Just as the living Father sent me, and I live because of the Father, so whoever eats me will live because of me. 58 This is the bread that came down from heaven, not like that which your ancestors ate, and they died. But the one who eats this bread will live forever." 59 He said these things while he was teaching in the synagogue at Capernaum. 60 When many of his disciples heard it, they said, "This teaching is difficult; who can accept it?" 61 But Jesus, being aware that his disciples were complaining about it, said to them, "Does this offend you? 62 Then what if you were to see the Son of Man ascending to where he was before? 63 It is the spirit that gives life; the flesh is useless. The words that I have spoken to you are spirit and life. 64 But among you there are some who do not believe." For Jesus knew from the first who were the ones that did not believe, and who was the one that would betray him. 65 And he said, "For this reason I have told you that no one can come to me unless it is granted by the Father." 66 Because of this many of his disciples turned back and no longer went about with him.

For the kingdom of God is not food and drink but righteousness and peace and joy in the Holy Spirit. 18 The one who thus serves Christ is acceptable to God and has human approval. 19 Let us then pursue what makes for peace and for mutual upbuilding. 20 Do not, for the sake of food, destroy the work of God. Everything is indeed clean, but it is wrong for you to make others fall by what you eat; 21 it is good not to eat meat or drink wine or do anything that makes your brother or sister[] stumble.[k] 22 The faith that you have, have as your own conviction before God. Blessed are those who have no reason to condemn themselves because of what they approve.

Twenty-five years ago, I completed a summer internship in Trenton, New Jersey. I lived in that city. I worked in that city. I ate in that city. At the corner of Hamilton and Tioga, right down from the church, there was a diner. Each morning, I would stop in to get the hottest coffee and the best old-fashioned donut one could find. I gobbled it up as I listened to their bemoaning the Phillies or their anticipating a better season for the Eagles with head coach Buddy Ryan. That little diner *was* Trenton: the food they ate, the topics they discussed, and the way they discussed it. I was dipped in it for four months. But after those four months, I needed something else for breakfast. I was missing something, actually yearning for something. I took my time getting back to Atlanta, spending nights with family up and down the east coast. Early one morning, not long after crossing over the North Carolina border, I pulled into Swannanoa Restaurant for breakfast.... more specifically, for a big bowl of grits.

I longed for grits. I yearned for grits. I guess it sounds silly. I guess I probably could've found some in an A&P or Foodtown there in Trenton, but I never tried. All I know is I couldn't get them at the diner. And all I know is that bowl of grits was like tasting home. When I gobbled up those grits, I was home.

One day in the spring of 1607, when sea weary members of the London Company came ashore at Jamestown, they were greeted by a band of friendly Indians offering bowls of a hot substance consisting of softened maize, seasoned with salt and some kind of animal fat. The welcomers called it "rockahominie." The settlers liked it so much they adopted it as part of their own diet. They set about devising a milling process by which the large corn grains could be ground into smaller particles without losing any nutrients. The experiment was a success and grits become a mainstay.[41]

In her book, *The Edible South*, Marcie Ferris says that, after the Civil War, the baseline of southern food was three things: meat, meal and molasses - what meat they could obtain (usually hog), what sugar they could grow, and what crop they could grind. Meat, meal and

---

[41] Charles Reagan Wilson and William Ferris, William, ed. <u>Encyclopedia of Southern Culture</u>. (Chapel Hill: UNC Press, 1989).

molasses.[42]   That was the southern diet after the war - for rich and poor, for black and white - for everyone.

Bill Neal studied southern food for years. To him, it has always boiled down to corn. "Every southerner knows the one item distinguishing his diet is corn. Fresh, dried or distilled. He may find hot biscuits in the Midwest or moist smoky hams in New England, but he won't find his hushpuppies, spoon bread or grits. The south has been steadfast in its loyalty to the native grain. Almost every other cuisine adapted wheat as the preferred bread-making staple, as soon as it became available. Southern cooks, though, held corn and its many breads in the highest regard. Not until the twentieth century do corn breads have close rival in the general diet."[43]

Neal continues. "Native North American would have found it heresy to question the supremacy of their staple crop. The word 'maize' connoted the idea of a universal mother who sustained life. The value of corn in North America has not diminished during the five thousand or so years of its cultivation. Exactly where and when corn appeared is not known. But man prized it enough to ensure its continuity. And the farmer is essential to the reproduction of corn. It is a crop dependent on agriculture. No wild corn has ever been found. No known corn can reseed itself. The early English settlers who frittered away their time in a futile search for gold would have done better to pursue the main achievement of Indian agriculture." Today in the United States corn remains a key crop. According to economist, it remains our most valuable crop, and the value of its annual harvest surpasses by far the product of all metal mined or coal extracted.[44]   Corn is key. Nikita Khrushchev once bemoaned to his comrades that "Americans are even masters of turning their corn into flakes!"[45]

No wonder I yearned for grits. Food is part of who we are and who we come to be. To know a place, you eat their food. To know a people, you eat their food. Certainly, it is different place to place, town to town,

---

[42] Marcie Cohen Ferris. <u>The Edible South: The Power of Food and the Making of an American Region</u>. (Chapel Hill: UNC Press, 2014).
[43] Bill Neal, <u>Southern Cooking</u>. (Chapel Hill: UNC Press, 1985).
[44] ibid.
[45] I read this somewhere, I forget now. I have it in a quote book.

home to home. You walk around a market in another part of the world, and you think, "Oh my gosh! What are they eating?!" You walk around Lexington Market in Baltimore, and you see them slapping together crab cakes. You walk around Pike Place in Seattle, and you will see more fish than you desire. You walk in the Piggly Wiggly in Elm City, and it is a biology class on boars... pig ears, pig feet, pig jowls, pig face! Your comfort level depends on whether it is your home or not.

Neal says that southern food is not simply food cooked south of Mason-Dixon Line. It is a product of time, people and place. From 1607 to 1860, three cultures - European, African and Native American - accepted and modified each other's agricultural dietary and social customs and molded them into something distinct. The cooking, like society it reflected, was never homogeneous, but it was a synthesis of the major forces behind it.[46]

To know a place, you eat their food. To know a people, you eat their food - country by country, region by region, even family by family. You know your grandmother's apply pie the moment it touches your tongue. Anthony Bourdain said that food is "an extension of nationalist feeling, ethnic feeling, your personal history, your province, your region, your tribe, your grandma. It's inseparable from those from the get-go."[47] Food is home.

You may not have considered it, but it is that way in Scripture too. The Israelites celebrated their deliverance every year with a meal. Still do. It is home ... reminding them who they are and how they were made. And it is precious ... reminding them of a time when food was scarce. Manna in the wilderness. Bread and fish on a hillside. God's people became anxious without it. Jesus knew all that. Jesus knew that food was precious. He knew the importance of bread. He knew it when he catered a meal for 5,000 people. At that moment, he said "I am the bread of life."

"I am the living bread that came down from heaven. Whoever eats this bread will live forever. This bread is my flesh, which I will give for the life of the world."

---

[46] ibid.

[47] Anthony Bourdain.
https://www.brainyquote.com/quotes/anthony_bourdain_552955

They thought he was nuts. "Do you know what you are saying?" He knew what he was saying. He knew it sounded odd. And he doubled down.

"Very truly I tell you, unless you eat the flesh of the Son of Man and drink his blood, you have no life in you. Whoever eats my flesh and drinks my blood has eternal life, and I will raise them up at the last day. For my flesh is real food and my blood is real drink. Whoever eats my flesh and drinks my blood remains in me, and I in them. Just as the living Father sent me and (just as) I live because of the Father, so the one who feeds on me will live because of me."

And then, the greatest understatement in the history of Scripture comes next. Verse 60, "The disciples responded, "This is a hard teaching." I'll say! It is a down-right bizarre teaching! You might even say it is an offensive teaching. "Does this offend you?" Jesus asks. At this point, according the scripture, people started jumping ship. "Many of the disciples then turned back and stopped following him." I bet.

It is hard. It is odd. It is not just odd to us. It was odd to them then. In fact, it was the basis for some of Rome's distaste for these 2nd century Christians. Rumors swirled that they were cannibals. Rome felt justified in persecuting them. So, this is a "hard learning." And we will not ever understand it until we understand food, until we understand difference between eating and consuming.

Jesus speaks in a way to generate some shock value, to get their attention. It is a symbolic way of speaking. Jesus did not mean to literally eat his flesh or drink his blood. This is why Biblical literalists will always have a hard time when they get to this point in the Bible. It is a symbolic way of speaking. At the same time, it should not be so quickly categorized and dismissed. Jesus is serious. For Jesus, it is about knowing why you eat. Do you eat to fill a hole? Do you eat because you are famished? Or do you eat so you might sustain, grow and live? And for Jesus it is about knowing what you eat. It is food to get by on or food to live on? We all need food to get by. That what manna was in the wilderness. It got them by to the next day. That is what the food was on the hillside in Galilee - enough fish and loaves to get them by a night. God provides all that too. It is a gift. But so is another kind of food - one that is *really* food, food that sustains and gives life. "My flesh is true food. My blood is true drink." And so, to *really* live, to *fully* experience life, one has to eat *real* food, one has to consume it, take it all in, make it part of you, recognize that it IS part of you.

Jesus IS that food, that *real* food, that *true* food that makes life happen. So to really live, to fully experience life as the people God called us to be, then we need to take him in, absorb him. Jesus is our home. He is the meal we yearn for when we have been away. He is the meal that comforts us, the meal that sustains us. He is the meal that connects us to our roots. He is the meal that connects us one to another - rich or poor, black or white, men or women. He is the meal that connects us generation to generation. He is the grain that can't be outsold, that grain that no one quite understands how it got here but can only say that it is a gift of God. He is the dish that comes to different people in a million different ways, but yet it remains the same. Everything comes back to him. He is our home. He is our grits! That is what Jesus means by food.

Have you ever thought how unique it is that one of our sacraments in our faith is a meal? A meal! A sacrament is an outward sign of an invisible grace. Conceivably, anything could have been a sacrament: making a pot, planting a tree, cutting your hair or tying a shoe. But our sacrament - one them - is a meal of all things. And the meal was bread- a bread of life.

Julia Child said once that "you can't be great, as a nation, as place, as home, if your bread taste like Kleenex."[48] There are all kinds of food, stuff to fill you and get you by. There is but one food that saves you, one that gives you life.

Thanks be to God.

---

[48] Noel Riley Fitch. <u>Appetite for Life: Biography of Julia Child</u>. (New York: Anchor, 1997).

What You Wear
Ephesians 6:10-20, Romans 13: 11-14

Finally, be strong in the Lord and in the strength of his power. [11] Put on the whole armor of God, so that you may be able to stand against the wiles of the devil. [12] For our struggle is not against enemies of blood and flesh, but against the rulers, against the authorities, against the cosmic powers of this present darkness, against the spiritual forces of evil in the heavenly places. [13] Therefore take up the whole armor of God, so that you may be able to withstand on that evil day, and having done everything, to stand firm. [14] Stand therefore, and fasten the belt of truth around your waist, and put on the breastplate of righteousness. [15] As shoes for your feet put on whatever will make you ready to proclaim the gospel of peace. [16] With all of these, take the shield of faith, with which you will be able to quench all the flaming arrows of the evil one. [17] Take the helmet of salvation, and the sword of the Spirit, which is the word of God. [18] Pray in the Spirit at all times in every prayer and supplication. To that end keep alert and always persevere in supplication for all the saints. [19] Pray also for me, so that when I speak, a message may be given to me to make known with boldness the mystery of the gospel, [20] for which I am an ambassador in chains. Pray that I may declare it boldly, as I must speak.

Besides this, you know what time it is, how it is now the moment for you to wake from sleep. For salvation is nearer to us now than when we became believers; [12] the night is far gone, the day is near. Let us then lay aside the works of darkness and put on the armor of light; [13] let us live honorably as in the day, not in reveling and drunkenness, not in debauchery and licentiousness, not in quarreling and jealousy. [14] Instead, put on the Lord Jesus Christ, and make no provision for the flesh, to gratify its desires.

There was a show on TV a few years ago: <u>What not to Wear</u>. Essentially, two fashion stylists would meet with some poor slob, review the person's sad wardrobe and then create a new look. They told these people what not to wear and what to wear. I never had thought much about it, but it is important. How you dress is important. Maybe you don't think it should be, but it is. It has been that way for a while. Mark Twain said once, that "clothes make the man." "Clothes make a man. Naked people have very little power in our society."

It's true. So we learn what to wear where and what not to wear anywhere. Context is key! We learn what to wear and what not to wear to a funeral. We learn what to wear and what not to wear to the first day of school, what to wear and what not to wear to the doctor's office, what to wear and what not to were climbing Mt. Everest. It does make a difference. Whether you like it or not, clothes make a man, make the woman.

A couple weeks ago, on a Saturday morning, I got up early to do some yard work. I had not showered or shaved. I was cutting grass and trimming bushes. After a while, I was a bit of a mess. About 11:00, Julie asked me to take a break and drive her to the Dollar General. I grabbed the keys and off we went. When we arrived, she said, "Listen. You just wait in the car. You can't go in there looking like that." And I thought, "Good gosh! How bad must I look that I can't go in the dollar store?!"

What one wears is important. Oddly enough, it is important in Ephesians. The Letter to the Ephesians was most likely written to many groups rather than to one specific group. It was written to a collection of early church communities with the intention that they would forward it to each other, like an ancient email forward. It was written to the church in a time of distress. These young churches were unexpectedly dealing with division with their ranks. It was a division of mistrust and resentment, of prejudice, a division that, in Paul's words, left them ... "separated from Christ, alienated from commonwealth, strangers to the covenant," a division that left them "without hope and without God." These churches were now also dealing with oppression, with a larger culture that did not always understand them and in some cases persecuted them. This was a new context for these young church communities. They were, in a manner of speaking, at war.

Now, this is not war detailed in history books. This is a spiritual battle. There is tension in community on the inside and pressure on the community from the outside. Inside division makes one vulnerable for outside attacks. So, the author reminds these church communities that these divisive ways make them vulnerable. The author reminds them that the context has changed. They are now in a spiritual battle. They are no longer in everyday mode. They should be in battle mode. Then, at the end of the letter, the author suddenly talks about what to wear. This might seem unusual, but when context changes the first thing to discuss, apparently, is what one wears. It is interesting that when it comes time to address powers of evil, the author chooses to talk about clothes. He could have talked strategy. He could have talked positioning and territory. He decides to talk about clothes. What to wear. Context is key.

So, what does one wear to battle? Business casual? That will not work. No, in a battle one needs armor. Except this is no ordinary battle. This is a completely different challenge. This is a *spiritual* battle. Now, for some, the concept of a "spiritual battle" might sound silly. It might sound soft, unlike military battles with tanks and bombers. We have learned how to fight military battles. We know what to wear for those battles and what tools are needed for those battles. We are not so clear what to wear for a spiritual battle. What does one wear to battle "the dark forces of this world?" What does one wear to contend against "the spiritual forces of evil in the heavenly realm?" Suddenly, we realize this is a big task. Suddenly, we realize this is a daunting foe. Suddenly, we can feel rather inadequate.

The television show taught me some lessons about dressing. There are rules. It is better to have too many layers than not enough. It is better to be cleaner than dirtier. It is better to be dressed up than dressed down. The rules make sense. There are reasons behind many of the rules. There might be social reasons - what to wear at a funeral or wedding. There might be professional reasons - what is expected at a job. There might be safety reasons - a life-vest on a boat, steel-toed boots at worksite. The reasons make sense. I noticed, though, that there is a basic concern with every rule. Inadequacy. The wrong dress could make you feel silly, out of place. The wrong dress could create a bad impression in this world based on first impressions. The wrong dress could get you killed.

Over the years, Christians have had some tendencies in our attempts to live out this passage and battle the "dark forces of the world," the "spiritual forces of evil in the heavenly realm." One, has been to not battle at all, but to take cover. It may be the most common tactic.

Facing "dark forces" is daunting. Addressing the "spiritual forces of evil in the heavenly realm" is unsettling. We generally don't have much confidence in ourselves and honestly, not much confidence in the Almighty as the Almighty wants us to have. So, we tend to take cover. Yet while that is the most common approach, it is also ineffective. And unfaithful.

The other approach is just the opposite. This approach takes seriously the call to dress appropriately for battle. Unfortunately, it fails in knowing how to dress. It is a battle, so one thinks armor. For centuries people wore armor to do battle. So using this scripture as a basis and looking at what others wore in battle, we armored ourselves in the fashion of the times: breastplate of iron, boots of steel, shields of platinum, helmets of graphite, and swords and spears of choice. Sadly, we learned this is inadequate and unfaithful too.

Do you remember the story of David and Goliath? In I Samuel the people of Israel face a difficult situation. The Philistines have come knocking once again. They have big, bad Goliath, an evil greater than any had ever seen. He is huge. He is well-defended: a helmet on his head, a shield around his chest, a cover across his legs, a javelin of bronze and a spear made of iron. Everything about him is overwhelming, even his speech. He challenges the nation of Israel.

The king of Israel is desperate for a warrior, but the people of Israel want nothing to do with Goliath. They are content to flee. The only one willing to stand up is David - little David, wholly inadequate David, who is not even the biggest of his family. David is the youngest of the eight sons of Jesse of Bethlehem. David isn't a warrior. He tends to sheep! Yet, he is the one who volunteers, so the king prepares David for battle. Moreover, the king prepares David for battle as a king would prepare for battle. The king attempts to outfit David in the weapons of war. If Goliath is wearing a bronze helmet, David needs a bronze helmet. If Goliath is covered in a coat of mail, David needs a coat of mail. If Goliath is carrying a sword, David needs a sword. But you know the story. David can't walk in it. It is too big, too heavy. It doesn't fit. He is over-dressed. So, David tells the king "No. I will not wear your armor." It just will not work. In fact, attempting to lumber around in this armor will only work against him! David sheds the conventional trappings and claims the tools made for him.

This brings me to Ephesians 6. Do not misinterpret Ephesians 6, as some Christians have been prone to do. This is not a permission to battle the world with the worlds' battle tools. We cannot do spiritual battle with such weapons. They will not fit. In fact, attempting to lumber around in that armor will only work against us! Ephesians 6 is, in fact, just the opposite. It offers a different dress: A breastplate of *righteousness*. Boots of *peace*. Shields of *faith*. Buckles of *truth*. Helmets of *salvation*. This a very different type of armor. This is a very different type of outfit. These are all defensive items, except one. The offensive tool is the "sword of the spirit, which is the Word of God," which is, by the way, Christ himself, the "Word of God." That weapon is Jesus Christ, who demonstrated a unique way to defeat enemies, whose words have a way of cutting both ways, of convicting your own life even as it convicts your enemies, and who is the only answer to evil and sin in this world. He is the only power to face the "dark forces of the world," the "spiritual forces of evil in the heavenly realm." That is the weapon we are given. That is what we wear.

During the Argentine military dictatorship from 1976 to 1983, something like 30,000 Argentine citizens, many of them young people, vanished. They were taken from their homes at night, arrested, interrogated, tortured, and never heard from again. They were called "The Disappeared." The families of these people could have buried themselves in fear. They could also have tried to use their kitchen utensils for tools and foolishly battle the regime on the regime's terms. They did neither. They went another route. For thirty years, the mothers and wives of these lost people gathered in the city square, right under the eyes and fist of their oppressive government, and they marched. They named themselves the "Mothers of the Plaza de Mayo." They would walk, in silence and great dignity. In some cases they would dance, alone, in the invisible arms of lost loved ones. Many had a unique dress for the occasion. (Context is key). Each wore a white head scarf in the form of a baby diaper, symbolizing their lost children. You might say, in the words of Ephesians, that they "put on the full armor of God, so that you can take your stand against the devil's schemes."

The musical artist Sting wrote a song about it.[49]

"Why are these women here dancing on their own?
Why is there this sadness in their eyes?
Why are the soldiers here? Their faces fixed like stone.
I can't see what it is they despise
It's the only form of protest they're allowed.
I've seen their silent faces scream so loud.
If they were to speak these words they'd go missing too.
Another woman on the torture table. what else can they do?

They're dancing with the missing. They're dancing with the dead.
They dance with the invisible ones. Their anguish is unsaid.
They're dancing with their fathers. They're dancing with their sons.
They're dancing with their husbands. They dance alone. They dance
alone.

Hey Mr. Pinochet. You've sown a bitter crop.
It's foreign money that supports you. One day the money's going to stop.
No wages for your torturers. No budget for your guns.
Can you think of your own mother Dancin' with her invisible son?

One day we'll dance on their graves. One day we'll sing our freedom.
One day we'll laugh in our joy. And we'll dance.
One day we'll dance on their graves.
One day we'll sing our freedom.
One day we'll laugh in our joy.
And we'll dance.

When asked them how the authorities, the forces, reacted, one lady said,

"At first they made fun of us and called us mad.
Then one day, they surrounded us.
They said they would shoot us if we didn't disperse. But we didn't
disperse.
We stood right there. One of the women fell to her knees, then another,

---

[49] Sumner, Gordon "Sting." "They Dance Alone." <u>Nothing Like the Sun</u>. A&M Records, 1988.

and then we all did, fell to our knees
and began to pray, 'Our Father who art in heaven. . ..'
And the soldiers lowered their weapons,
got back in their little trucks
and drove away.'[50]

What you wear matters. Because what you wear protects you. And because it says something about you, and because it makes you. Clothes make the man, make the woman.

Thanks be to God.

---

[50] Notes from Rev. John Buchanan's visit to Argentina with the PCUSA group. Fourth Presbyterian Church Chicago, IL, 2006.

What You Do
John 21:1-19, James 1: 22-25

After these things Jesus showed himself again to the disciples by the Sea of Tiberias; and he showed himself in this way. ²Gathered there together were Simon Peter, Thomas called the Twin, Nathanael of Cana in Galilee, the sons of Zebedee, and two others of his disciples. ³Simon Peter said to them, "I am going fishing." They said to him, "We will go with you." They went out and got into the boat, but that night they caught nothing.

⁴Just after daybreak, Jesus stood on the beach; but the disciples did not know that it was Jesus. ⁵Jesus said to them, "Children, you have no fish, have you?" They answered him, "No." ⁶He said to them, "Cast the net to the right side of the boat, and you will find some." So they cast it, and now they were not able to haul it in because there were so many fish. ⁷That disciple whom Jesus loved said to Peter, "It is the Lord!" When Simon Peter heard that it was the Lord, he put on some clothes, for he was naked, and jumped into the sea. ⁸But the other disciples came in the boat, dragging the net full of fish, for they were not far from the land, only about a hundred yards off. ⁹When they had gone ashore, they saw a charcoal fire there, with fish on it, and bread. ¹⁰Jesus said to them, "Bring some of the fish that you have just caught." ¹¹So Simon Peter went aboard and hauled the net ashore, full of large fish, a hundred fifty-three of them; and though there were so many, the net was not torn. ¹²Jesus said to them, "Come and have breakfast." Now none of the disciples dared to ask him, "Who are you?" because they knew it was the Lord. ¹³Jesus came and took the bread and gave it to them and did the same with the fish. ¹⁴This was now the third time that Jesus appeared to the disciples after he was raised from the dead. ¹⁵When they had finished breakfast, Jesus said to Simon Peter, "Simon son of John, do you love me more than these?" He said to him, "Yes, Lord; you know that I love you." Jesus said to him, "Feed my lambs." ¹⁶A second time he said to him, "Simon son of John, do you love me?" He said to him, "Yes, Lord; you know that I love you." Jesus said to him, "Tend my sheep." ¹⁷He said to him the third time, "Simon son of John, do you love me?" Peter felt hurt because he said to him the third time, "Do you love me?" And he said to him, "Lord, you know everything; you know that I love you." Jesus said to him, "Feed my sheep. ¹⁸Very truly, I tell you, when you were younger, you used to fasten your own belt and to go wherever you wished. But when you grow old, you will stretch out your hands, and someone else will fasten a belt around you and take you where you do not wish to go." [19] (He said this to indicate the kind of death by which he would glorify God.) After this he said to him, "Follow me."

But be doers of the word, and not merely hearers who deceive themselves. [23] For if any are hearers of the word and not doers, they are like those who look at themselves[L] in a mirror; [24] for they look at themselves and, ongoing away, immediately forget what they were like. [25] But those who look into the perfect law, the law of liberty, and persevere, being not hearers who forget but doers who act— they will be blessed in their doing.

The Gospels are of course, first and foremost, the story of Jesus Christ. So, please do not mistake what I am saying. The gospels are about Jesus, primarily. Still, it is also fair to say that, in another way, the gospels are about the disciples. The gospels are about those people who followed Jesus. Even if secondarily, the gospels tell the story of these average men and women who, against better judgment, went after Jesus, who left their jobs and walked after him. What propelled them? What shaped them? What changed them? What changed *in* them? For they *were* changed. They began as fishermen, most of them, by the Sea of Galilee. Jesus says, "follow me." They dropped their nets and followed. Again, we don't know what specifically moved them, if they were taken by the Spirit, if they had heard things about Jesus, if they were looking for a chance to leave home, or all of the above. We just know that they left their jobs and Jesus became their job.

Today's scripture is at the end of the Gospel of John. And the end of John's Gospel is almost a full-circle moment. The story ends where it began, by the sea. Jesus began his ministry by coming to the sea and calling these fishermen. Jesus curiously ends his ministry also by the sea, calling the fishermen to come ashore. Where earlier, they were on the shore mending nets, in the hopes of finding fish. Here, they are on a boat, hauling in a load of fish, thanks to Jesus. Where earlier, they didn't know him. Now, none of them dared ask who he was "for they all knew who he was." Full circle. It ends, where it began. Yet, they have been changed. They are different people. They have a new job. They have a vocation.

Vocation is a big word in the history of Christian faith - not vacation, but vocation. Vacation is a time away from what you do. Vocation is what you do. Now, vocation is not just your job. Vocation is a purpose. It is the thing you were made to be and do. In Christian thought, there are *specific* vocations (painter, plumber, doctor, dentist, etc) and there are *general* vocations. General vocations are those that fall upon anyone who follows the man from Nazareth. Karl Barth said that "The call of Jesus Christ is decisively an invitation and demand that the men to whom it comes should adopt a particular inward and outward line of action and conduct of which we have the basic form in the two fold command to love God and our neighbors and a normative description in the imperatives of the sermon on the mount. The Christian is the man or woman who gladly accepts this invitation and demand as a binding word of the Lord and stirs himself to obey and to do justice to it. He is essentially a 'doer' of the word of Jesus Christ, who calls him to a new order and orientation of his life."[51] To unpack that a bit: The Christian is one who accepts Christ' invitation, who takes that call as binding and who then allows Christ's words to affect who he or she is and how he or she is in the world. The Christian is essentially a "doer of the word." Thus... it is what you do.

People forget, but "what we do" is a big deal. Little kids get asked "what are you going to do when you grow up?" High School Seniors get asked, "what are you going to do next year?" College graduates get asked, "what are you do with that degree?" It never stops. Soldiers out of the service: "What are you going to do now?" Men and women getting ready to retire: "What are you going to do now?" You can't do nothing. You have to do something. What are you going to do?

My father is an engineer. He IS an engineer. He has been retired for several years, yet he is still an engineer. He knew he was going to be one when he was seven. He was an engineer his whole life. When he retired - the first time - he went home, played golf and after about three minutes he went back to work. What we do has a hold on us. It is how we understand ourselves. What we do shapes and makes us. What we do is often the first thing people say about us. "This is John, he is a teacher. This is Sally, she is a banker. This is Fred, he is a farmer. This

---

[51] Karl Barth, Church Dogmatics, vol IV. part 3.2. (Edinburgh: T&T Clark, 1956-1975), 559.

is Sue, she is an actress. This is Joe, he works at the DMV. This is Jane, she works at home." Everybody has something they do.

We are what we do. So it is not unusual for people to have hard time when they don't do what they do -when the engineer retires, when the solider comes home, when the athlete hangs up his cleats. How many athletes try to come back for a second chance? Jim Palmer, Michael Jordan, Brett Favre, Gordie Howe? It doesn't always go well. Richard Petty retired from NASCAR in 1991. Three years later, he was charged with reckless driving for bumping a vehicle in front of him on I-85! We are what we do.

So... what do we do when we can't do what we do? It is hard to know what to do if we no longer do what we did! I think that is what is happening to the disciples in this scripture. Look at the beginning of Chapter 21. Jesus has just been raised from the dead! It is the culmination of the gospel! He was dead. Now he is alive! The tomb is empty. The strife is over. The victory is won! So obviously the next question for the disciples is "So disciples, what are you going to do now?" "Eeh, I guess we will go fishing." "What? fishing? You are going fishing? That is all you can come up with?" You might think on the heels of the resurrection the disciples would through a big party or run through the streets singing or run down to the Sanhedrin doing an I-told-you-so dance. But no, not here. They go back to what they did before. They go back to fishing. They go back to fishing because they are fishermen! It is what they do! "Jesus is risen. Ok. Great. What do we do now? Gosh, hmm...well, I guess we could go fishing. We *are* fishermen."

They fished all night, but they had no luck. The fish weren't biting. It is that way sometimes, despite our best efforts. A voice calls out from the shore. "Try the other side of the boat." Odd, but fishermen are always looking for suggestions, so they do what he says to do. They toss their empty net on the other side *and...* you know the story. It is a Fish Story for the generations, a haul too heavy to haul, more fish than ever fished. But we all know that the story is not just about fishing, right? It isn't about how to cast or how to bait a hook. We all know these fishermen are not just fisherman, right? We can see that this story of guys going fishing after the resurrection isn't simply about guys going fishing after the resurrection, right? We all know that the miracle is not just about fish, right? It is not just a story about Jesus helping the guys catch a bunch of fish. There is something deeper going on here. The message is NOT that Jesus will make you better at your job. It is more like, there is more to you *than* your job or there is more to your job than your *job*!

These are fishermen, yes. They have a day job. They fish. But they have another job. You might say they are moonlighting. They have a *vocation*. They catch people now. They might be fishermen, but now, now their identity is *more* than being fishermen. There is more to them than their job. They are known by their vocation.

For as much as we do it, there are many problems for staking our identities on our jobs. The primary one is that your job can be taken away from you. You could lose your job, or you spend a bunch of money on college and can't find one, or you get into it and figure out it isn't for you, or you start it and find out you hate it, or there is an accident and you can't do it, or you work it for thirty years and get fired from it, or you work it for fifty years and retire from it. Then what? Then who are you?

Joe Gibbs coached the Washington Redskins for a long time. He was very successful. He won two Super Bowls. Then, one day, he quit. He decided to race cars. "Why are you doing that?" He said this. "Well, when you do something for a long period of time, you actually look at it and say, 'What else is out there?' I coached football and had some measure of success. What am I really going to do? Do it again? I think with some people, at some point in life, they say to themselves, 'Maybe there's something else out there. Maybe there is something else that I would like to do.' For me, success really came down to having the right priorities in life. If you think about that, should my occupation -- making money -- be the first thing in my life? I don't think so. My priority, first, has always be God. And everything else follows." And that gave him a freedom. John Calvin said once, years ago, "No task will be so sordid and base, provided you obey your calling in it, that it will not shine and be reckoned very precious in God's sight."[52]

The story of the disciples begins by the sea. It ends by the sea too. At the beginning of the Gospel, they are fisherman. At the end of the Gospel, they are something more. They are more than even fishermen.

On the beach, Jesus talks to Peter. "Simon son of John, do you love me more than these?" Simon Peter said, "Yes, Lord; you know that I love you." Jesus said, "Feed my lambs." Jesus said to him, again, "Simon son of John, do you love me?" Simon Peter said to him, "Yes, Lord; you know that I love you." Jesus said, "Tend my sheep." Jesus said to him, the third time, "Simon son of John, do you love me?" Simon Peter felt hurt because he said to him the third time, "Do you love me?" And Simon Peter said to him, "Lord, you know everything; you know that I love you." Jesus said to him, "Feed my sheep.

Three times, he addresses Peter. He gives Peter an opportunity to redeem himself, after the three times Peter denied him in the courtyard. Three times Jesus asks him about love. Three times Peter affirms his love. Three times Jesus tells him what loving Jesus back means. He doesn't speak of belief, though belief is inferred. He speaks of doing something. He speaks of what you DO. He tells him what to DO. "You love me? Really? Ok, then, this is what you DO!" And suddenly, they aren't just catching fish. They are tending to sheep. So in effect, these fishermen are not just fishermen anymore. They are shepherds! They have a new job! They have a vocation! Their vocation is to shepherd God's people.

Whatever you do, do what you do. But remember, you are more than your job. You too have a vocation, a calling to which we were all called. The Christian is the man or woman who gladly accepts this call, this invitation, this demand as a binding word, and stirs himself or herself to obey and to do justice to it. We are 'doers' of the word of Jesus Christ. Questions remain and will pop up. They are repeated in Scripture, again and again, "What must I *do* to be saved? What must I

[52] Jeff Haden, "Redefining Success: One-one-One with NFL and NASCAR Legend Joe Gibbs. https://www.inc.com/jeff-haden/redefining-success-one-on-one-with-nfl-and-nascar-legend-joe-gibbs.html

do to have eternal life? What must we *do* to do works of God? What must we *do*? The answers become repetitive as well. Believe in the Him. And feed His sheep. No matter your job.

Amen.

New Neighbors
John 14: 1-8

"Do not let your hearts be troubled. Believe in God, believe also in me. ²In my Father's house there are many dwelling places. If it were not so, would I have told you that I go to prepare a place for you? ³And if I go and prepare a place for you, I will come again and will take you to myself, so that where I am, there you may be also. ⁴And you know the way to the place where I am going." ⁵Thomas said to him, "Lord, we do not know where you are going. How can we know the way?" ⁶Jesus said to him, "I am the way, and the truth, and the life. No one comes to the Father except through me. ⁷If you know me, you will know my Father also. From now on you do know him and have seen him."

A few things might have changed on Poole Road. The thirty minute drive from Raleigh to the small town of Wendell on this two-lane will take you by Paul Lee's Grocery, Tilton's Auto Yard, five middle-class subdivisions, the Bethlehem Baptist Church, rows and rows of tobacco fields and one Buddhist temple. Clearly, a few things have changed on Poole Road. There is a Buddhist temple between Tilton's Auto Yard and the Bethlehem Baptist Church.

In the past thirty years, the religious landscape of America is radically transformed. "The United States is the most religiously diverse nation in the world."[53] For some people this are welcome news. For others it is disturbing or unsettling. Some see religious pluralism as a threat and react with concern and, in some cases, discrimination.[54] Others see religious pluralism as an ideal and seek to support and encourage it.[55] Many, many others seem content to drive on by, on to Sunday School for the same lesson, not quite sure what to think… or not thinking much about it at all. But there it is, between Tilton's Auto Yard and the Bethlehem Baptist Church and, at some point, questions emerge. How does one reconcile the Gospel's lean claim of Christ as THE way in a world plump with many ways?

---

[53] Diane Eck, <u>A New Religious America</u> (New York: HarperSanFrancisco, 2001), 1.
[54] Eck, 295; and Religionlink.org, "Religious Discrimination Complaints Spike," Religion Newswriters Foundation, April 23, 2003.
[55] I am thinking of organizations like Pluralism Project of Harvard University and the Ontario Consultants on Religious Tolerance.

I tend to avoid controversial topics. I like my job. Perhaps it is a matter of self-preservation. Some topics you cannot avoid, though, particularly when Scripture takes you there. "I am the way the truth and the life. No one comes to the father but through me." That is a pretty lean claim. There doesn't seem to be much wiggly room there. It is easy to affirm inside the church walls. Once you leave, though, it is different.

It may not be a problem for you. It is a problem for many. It was a problem for Marvin Coghill, for those of you who remember him. Marvin was no liberal. Yet Marvin traveled all around the globe with his tobacco work, meeting, as he told me, good people of all kinds of faiths. He had trouble with the lean claims in a world plump of options. One might think that in Eastern North Carolina we are at a safe distance from it. I used to think so. But you only have to open your eyes. I went to lunch at the new Ti restaurant behind Wendy's. I walked in and there was a row of Tibetan monks performing an ancient rite, complete with chanting and tambourines. Water suddenly began to fall. Thinking the sprinkler system had gone off, I turned to exit. I paused as I was greeted by a very welcoming man shaking some scented water on me with a big sponge. My friend said, "I think you just got Buddha baptized."

I did my doctoral work on this topic. My theory was that secondary level students from Presbyterian churches leave for college with little or no preparation for the religiously plural campuses they are attending. I wanted to find a way to prepare them for that reality. I wanted to engage freshman as to how they were equipped for the campus and then to provide a guide for churches. I met with a handful of NC State freshmen from our area. What I discovered, though, was that these kids were not unfamiliar with religious diversity. Every one of the students I interviewed had, in their middle and high school years, lived, studied, played with kids of various other faiths - or no faith at all! The other thing I noticed was that, when faced with that fact, kids went one of two ways. Either they stayed true to a faith, but in a very exclusive, isolated way - finding a faith community that distrusts anyone outside its particular doors, including other Christians who might believe slightly differently than them, OR they move to a wide-open, inclusive place that is so relativistic that everything and anything goes and Jesus makes little difference at all. I longed for some wisdom in between.

Of course, this isn't a local topic. Christian thinkers have been wrestling with this for several years. When faced this issue, when faced with the issue of how one reconciles the Gospel's lean claims of Christ as the way of salvation in a world plump with a diversity of religious truth, there have generally been three answers: exclusivism, pluralism and inclusivism.

In short order, it goes like this.[56] *Exclusivist*s will tell you that Jesus is the way, the truth and the life, and there is no other name, way or truth. That means that however kindly you say it, Christians tell non-Christians that the Christian religion (or our version of it) is the one, true religion and all the others are false; that we have the truth and you don't; that our way of life is right, yours is wrong; that we have light and you grope in darkness; that God is for us and God is against you. *Inclusivists* will tell you that yes, Christ is the way, truth and the life, but God's grace can be at work in others of other faiths. So when you see Hindus or Muslims being Christian-like, they are encompassed in the story and are sort of anonymous Christians. *Pluralists* will tell you that for us Christians, Jesus is the way, truth and life, but there are also other paths to God. They will tell you that we Christians have experienced God in Christ, but others found the same thing in other ways. Jesus is one way, but not the only way. Those have seemed to be our choices. Good Christians will find themselves in any one of these. In my mind, though, none of them are very palatable.

Pluralism can seem the most intelligible and modern, but it fails in many ways. It dismisses the important particulars of the faith – of all faiths - and blurs them in a kind of lowest common denominator truth. Pluralists are not really pluralists in that they dismiss what makes us plural! Moreover, pluralism cloaks itself in this veil of objectivity. One scholar says, "It takes the position of an arbitrator of ultimate truth. The *real* reality is that reality that only the pluralist, with his or her

---

[56] This whole section is guided by Shirley C. Guthrie Jr, <u>Always Being Reformed; Faith for a Fragmented World</u> (Louisville: WJKP, 1996).

position above all the 'great religions,' is able to perceive."[57] *Inclusivism* has a similar problem. The inclusivists are not really inclusive because they don't really include others, as much as they try to make them something they are not. The idea that others are "anonymous Christians" is rather condescending and patronizing. It is saying, "We know you think you are a Buddhist, but really you are a Christian too. You just don't know any better!" *Exclusivists* are an easy mark these days, particularly in a world of political correctness. Still, you can't avoid the rather stark blinders of this position. Worse than the harshness, though, is the fact that exclusivist essentially exclude God. They dismiss the sovereignty of God by limiting the Almighty to their own positions, their theological worldview. They seem more interested in who is "in" than those left "out." They are more interested in superior wisdom, virtue and privilege than Christ himself. All of these, in my mind, are weak and insufficient.[58]

At one point in the early church, Paul brought the story of the Gospel to Athens. Athens was no religious backwater. Athens was a cosmopolitan place. Athens was full of smart people, a variety of religions, a cross-spectrum of beliefs (and non-beliefs), a thirst for enterprise and commerce, a drive for technology and competition, a love of art and sport, and a whole bunch of people! You know this

---

[57] Douglas John Hall, "Confessing Christ in the Pluralistic Context" in <u>Many Voices, One God: Being Faithful in a Pluralistic World</u>. ed George W. Stroup (Louisville: WJKP, 1998) 72. He goes on to say that "Pluralism may seem terribly urbane, and it is undoubtedly a needed corrective to religious provincialism and excessive subjectivity. In the end, however, it is all too predictably a child of modernity, serving faithfully the purpose of an academia whose evident desire is to avoid religious choices and involvement while playing the role of the disinterested and wise discerner of human religious behavior."

[58] From this perspective, it is faithful to stand with exclusivists in affirming the centrality of Christ for salvation, but less so when they seek to limit the freedom of God, the grace of Christ, and the breadth of the Spirit, who is known to move among those of other religions or no religion. It is faithful to stand with pluralists in affirming the work of the Triune God in people other than the church, but less so when they seek to dismiss important differences, and piously stand over and above those of any faith. It is faithful to stand with inclusivists in affirming the work of God in those who may not be aware of it, but not with them when they seek to patronize others.

kind of place. Yet, if one looks back at Paul's preaching in the city Athens, a few things become apparent. He preaches to a crowd of variety of beliefs. He preaches without violence and cruel hostility. He preaches without hesitation. He preaches matter-of-factly. He preaches, you might say, as confession - confession in the truest sense of the word, not as an apology, but as a "this is what I know." And this might be our very model for navigating faith in a pluralistic world - not in hostility, not in defensiveness, but as simple affirmation. "This is what I know. This is what I am coming to know."

What we confess is Jesus Christ. That is it. Nothing else. That is the truth of the world, of who God is. We find salvation and hope is in Christ. So, when approaching matters of religious diversity, we don't point to our religion or our faith. Goodness knows, we don't point to ourselves. And we don't point to how we do things, what we think, how we live or even what we believe. We point to Christ. "Come and see." Karl Barth was a preeminent Christian thinker in the 20th century. In the last full volume of his famous theological work, he wrote these words: "The statement that Jesus Christ is the one word of God has nothing to do with the arbitrary exaltation and glorification of the Christian in relation to other people, or the church in relation to other institutions or of Christianity in relation to other conceptions." [59] In other words, to be a Christian is to exalt and glorify Jesus Christ, not Christianity in general or the Christianity of any particular church.

We like to label people. We like to pigeonhole them. So, if you were forcing me to choose which of the three camps I belonged, I suppose you could put me in the exclusivist camp. Jesus is the way. That might sound harsh, but every religion makes a claim on spiritual truth.[60] That is the nature of religions. It may sound exclusive, but I am an exclusivist on a number of things. I think I am right about BBQ. I think I am right about SEC football. I think I am right about the designated hitter rule in baseball. People fall out in different places on those too, and we still manage to live together. So put me in the

---

[59] Karl Barth, Church Dogmatics, vol IV/3 (Edinburgh: T&T Clark, 1961), 91.
[60] Schubert Ogden, Is There Only One True Religion or Are There Many? (Dallas: Southern Methodist University, 1992) 11. "Every religion at least implicitly claims to be the true religion. It is part of the very nature of religion to claim authority on the meaning of ultimate reality."

exclusivist camp, if you want, and you can be in any one you want to, I suppose. But if you stick me there, know that I also affirm a couple things.

First, I know that there are others in this world who believe differently and that doesn't concern me one bit.[61] Not unlike ancient Athens, there are many faiths in play. In fact, for most of the history of the world, Christians have been one among many out there, with competing truth claims. Why do we think everyone has to look, think, believe just like us? We just tell our story. And the story we tell, according to Douglas John Hall, " is one whose veracity and import I can neither prove nor force anyone else to accept, indeed, is one whose depth of meaning I must myself continue to ponder and wrestle with; it is in short, a matter of faith, not sight."[62]

Second. Positioning myself behind Jesus as the only "way, truth and life," does not make me against the world, but honestly quite the opposite.[63] In fact, it is precisely Jesus that compels me to be open to the other person, which I would never do otherwise! The confessional claim of Christ as the way of salvation does not move the church away from the world. Quite the contrary, the church is called *to* the other, *for*

---

[61] Stanley Hauerwas, The State of the University, (Malden, MA: Blackwell, 2007), 61. Hauerwas argues that the existence of other faiths is nothing new. He says, "for some reason Christians in our time seem to think that the existence of other traditions presents a decisive challenge to the truth and intelligibility of the Christian faith. I confess I simply do not understand why they seem to assume that what we believe is problematic unless everyone believes what we believe. As far as I can see there is no biblical reason for such a view. Indeed, as I will suggest below, Christian scripture, and in particular the tower of Babel, implies that we should expect difference."

[62] Hall, 75.

[63] Douglas John Hall, Why Christian? (Nashville: Fortress, 1998), p.145. "I know that my own "natural" tendency, which has been reinforced by my familial, national, racial, class and other background, is to look upon all or nearly all of these "others " with a kind of half-conscious suspicion, or at least a certain caution. What continues to counteract and transform this aboriginal exclusivity of mine is chiefly... Jesus Christ. Far from sanctioning or encouraging the "natural" habit of exclusion, the grace that comes from the Source constantly judges that habit, and strives to replace it with at least the beginnings of a far greater openness to others... greater, indeed, than I usually find comfortable. If I am not the chauvinist, bigot, sexist, racist and so on that I might otherwise have been it is chiefly because of the Nazarene."

the other. Shirley Guthrie puts it this way: "In short, Jesus Christ is the way, the truth and the life of the Triune God who is not only present and at work among and for the sake of Christians, but present and at work among and for the sake of all people everywhere, even people of other religious faiths, people of no religious faith and, who knows, maybe even fellow Christians for whom we have contempt because they are too liberal, too conservative, or too pietistic in what they believe and too tradition shattering in the way they live."[64]

While we are being confessional, while we are saying what we believe, I'll also tell you this. Yes, Jesus Christ is the way and truth and life, and no one comes to Father but through him. It all comes through Christ. That means that it does not come through Christianity or my understanding of Christianity. It does not come through some scheme or some formula or some "plan of salvation" someone crafted out of the Bible, but only through Christ. Because of Christ, salvation is possible in this world, the Christ we know who loved the outcaste and the broken, the Christ who repeatedly bereted the religious insiders and forever welcomed the "outsiders." It is by HIS wisdom, HIS heart, HIS decision, HIS grace, that there is life for anyone. Under his grace, we are all dependent.

Some student asked my theology profession once what will God say, on that great day of reckoning, to all those poor people who do not believe - to all those Muslims, those Hindus, those Buddhists, and not just them but all those atheists or anyone else who isn't "on board." What will God say to them? My professor shook his head and said, "I don't know what God will say to them. But I know what God will say to us. God will turn to us and ask, 'Why don't they believe? Why don't they know? Why do they feel abandoned? Why have they not felt the love of God? Where was your example? How come your demonstration of the Gospel in the public arena was such that they were more repelled by it than drawn to it? Why did you make it about you and not about Christ?"

My son Jack has three friends in our neighborhood. Noah. Malachi. Yusuf. One is Jewish. One is Muslim. One is evangelical Christian.

---

[64] Guthrie, 70-71.

Except that they are around the same age, they have very little in common. Three of them have Biblical names: Noah. Malachi and Yusuf - Joseph. Of course my kid, the Presbyterian kid, doesn't. Jackson Lee. His name was inspired by two confederate generals. These boys have nothing in common, except that they are 10-year-old boys who want to play together. They go outside. They go outside, and they play war. Such is life. We want to be together and we can't help fighting. What do I think about it? Jesus is the way, the truth and the life, and he loves the little children, all the children of the world.

Thanks be to God.

Meeting the New Neighbors
John 14: 20-22, Acts 17: 22-28

20 On that day you will know that I am in my Father, and you in me, and I in you. 21 They who have my commandments and keep them are those who love me; and those who love me will be loved by my Father, and I will love them and reveal myself to them." 22 Judas (not Iscariot) said to him, "Lord, how is it that you will reveal yourself to us, and not to the world?"

22 Then Paul stood in front of the Areopagus and said, "Athenians, I see how extremely religious you are in every way. 23 For as I went through the city and looked carefully at the objects of your worship, I found among them an altar with the inscription, 'To an unknown god.' What therefore you worship as unknown, this I proclaim to you. 24 The God who made the world and everything in it, he who is Lord of heaven and earth, does not live in shrines made by human hands, 25 nor is he served by human hands, as though he needed anything, since he himself gives to all mortals life and breath and all things. 26 From one ancestor he made all nations to inhabit the whole earth, and he allotted the times of their existence and the boundaries of the places where they would live, 27 so that they would search for God and perhaps grope for him and find him—though indeed he is not far from each one of us. 28 For 'In him we live and move and have our being'; as even some of your own poets have said, 'For we too are his offspring.'

Following last week's sermon on religious pluralism, I received a great deal of feedback - some in agreement, some in disagreement. I also received reports of your own experiences. Your son dates a Jewish girl. You do business with a Hindu. Your office mate is an Atheist. This is not only a political issue or an academic question. This is real life. This is the world we live in, even here in Eastern North Carolina. Yet, while it is one thing to talk about what we *think*, it is another thing altogether to talk about what we *do*. It is one thing to figure out what one believes. It is a whole other thing to begin to live with folks who see the world quite differently. That is what I want to talk about today - not what we *think* about what someone else believes, but how we *relate* to them and how we might God working in them as well.

Living as a Christian in a religiously plural world can be a bit awkward. We do not always know what to say or how to be. Siding on tolerance, do we give away too much to be authentic? Choosing to be unyielding, do we give up any possibility of discovery? How are we to be? What are we to say?

In the academic world in recent years, the answer is *dialogue*. It is one of the more recent buzzwords. In this religiously plural context, scholars say, respectful, mutual conversation, "dialogue," is the appropriate Christian response. It is not haughty. It is not paternalistic. It is mutual and educational. It is the right response to this religiously plural world, to engage in very deliberate and intentional acts of interreligious dialogue, to sit down at tables, to listen and converse, to exchange ideas and grapple with each other as we grapple with truth.[65] Honestly though, I don't even know what that means.

It reminds me of a great story from Stanley Hauerwas. He was giving a lecture given at Hendrix College in Conway, Arkansas. The lecture involved, as he describes it, "why Christians, if we are to be Christians, owe it to ourselves and our neighbors to quit fudging our belief that God matters." At the conclusion of the lecture, a professor in the religion department expressed concern. The professor noted that such a stress on the centrality of Christian particulars provided "no theory that would enable Christians to talk with Buddhists." Hauerwas responds thusly, "If you want to talk with them (Buddhists) what good will a theory do you? I assume that if you want to talk with Buddhists, you would just go talk with them. You might begin by asking, for example, 'what in the world are you guys doing in Conway?' He then suggested that he suspected that the real challenge in Conway was not talking with the few Buddhists but trying to talk with Christian fundamentalists."[66]

I did my doctoral work on this topic. In the course of it, I found something very curious. This is what these college students had been doing all along. No one was initiating round tables of deliberate dialogue. Nonetheless, students were constantly engaged in pointed

[65] David Lochhead, <u>The Dialogical Imperative: A Christian Reflection on Interfaith Encounter,</u> (Maryknoll, NY: Orbis Books, 1988), 2.
[66] Hauerwas, <u>The State of The University,</u> (Malden: Blackwell Publishing, 2007), 58.

conversations on very personal religious topics, and without help from all of us so-very-wise adults. They were engaged in "dialogue," even if never called it that. They were just asking questions of each other. "Do you celebrate Christmas? What is Ramadan? Why do you eat that stuff?" In some cases, the questions were rather blunt. "I didn't know how else to ask it, so I just said, "why do you wear that thing on your head?"[67] These students had begun dialogue without any professional training! Again and again, students revealed straight-forward and, in some cases, intimate conversations with people of other faiths. The range was broad. I recall one pre-med student who worked afternoons in a hair salon. She seemed genuinely curious about other faiths and was willing to engage in respectful conversation. She was surprised, though, when her own faith was questioned. "I started talking to her more. And then she explained how it is different, how they worry that *we* are not going to heaven because of *our* beliefs. She said she was praying for me! I told her, 'But I was praying for you first!'"

I guess one might call all this "dialogue." I don't know. I do know it happens all the time, and it happens without a theory or a plan. People want to be in opportunities for spiritual growth without them becoming spiritual mine fields. They often want to know how to do so without being a heel or being a sap. How does one thoughtfully engage another person of faith about their faith? They also often want to know how they might discern where God could be at work in a world they do not understand. These are the two questions. How can I engage another person of faith while also staying to true to my own and how can I discern where God is at work in that other place, that other faith? I'll attempt to answer both of these questions

As far as the first question, thankfully, there is some help in an old catechism of the church. Years ago, some bright minds drafted Question 52 of the Study Catechism of the PC (USA):

How should I treat non-Christians and people of other religions?

---

67 Tom Watkins, "Preparing High School Graduates for the Religiously Plural Campus." DMin Dissertation. Union Presbyterian Seminary, 203.

As much as I can, I should meet friendship with friendship, hostility with kindness, generosity with gratitude, persecution with forbearance, truth with agreement, and error with truth. I should express my faith with humility and devotion as the occasion requires, whether silently or openly, boldly or meekly, by word or by deed. I should avoid compromising the truth on the one hand and being narrow-minded on the other. In short, I should always welcome and accept these others in a way that honors and reflects the Lord's welcome and acceptance of me.[68]

In summary, we react to others with the heart of Christ. If we remember, says one teacher, "who Jesus and the Triune God revealed in him are, we cannot look at people of other faiths or different understandings of the Christian faith as our enemies or enemies of our God. We can only recognize them as fellow human beings who, just like us, are created in the image of God, people who, like us, are loved and care for by God; people for whom, just as for us, Christ lived, died and rose again, people who are also promised the life renewing spirit of God. Moreover, if we know that when we go to meet them, we do not go into foreign territory, but into territory where the living, triune God has already been at work before we get there." That is the heart of Christ.

As far was being able to discern where God is at work in this world among a wide variety of people and faiths, that is a little more difficult. One has to take another step. In order to see this faithfully, one needs to seek to have the Mind of Christ. If the Christian wants to know where God is at work and where God is not at work in the world, then the Christian first needs to carefully consider the identity and ministry of Christ. Where do we see God 's work in the world? We look for the evidence. We look for God's fingerprints. Nothing has guided me more here than Shirley Guthrie's insight in a book entitled *Always Being Reformed: Faith for a Fragmented World.* [69] Guthrie offers the following wisdom.

Wherever and among whomever physical life is treated with respect and tended to responsibly (including the material life of animals, plants, water and air), we may gratefully recognize the presence and work of the God whom Christians confess to be the world's creator. On the other hand,

---

[68] The Study Catechism, Presbyterian Church (USA), 1998.
[69] Guided by Shirley C Guthrie Jr, Always Being Reformed; Faith for a Fragmented World (Louisville: WJKP, 1996).

wherever and among whomever (including among Christians) there is indifference toward or contempt for such things, there is exposed a lack of faith in and indeed opposition to the God who created it.

Wherever and among whomever the dignity and value of human life is respected and protected (in personal relationships or in public policy) then we may gratefully recognize the presence and work of the Creator. On the other hand, wherever and among whomever (including among Christians) there is indifference toward or aggression toward any human life, then the God we Christians confess is absent.

Wherever and among whomever we see religion and morality with characteristics of seeking to befriend the rejected, invite the excluded, love without qualification, seek justice for the broken, and reconcile the divided then we may recognize the presence and work of the God we know in Christ. Wherever religion and morality are motivated by love of God and fellow humans rather than a self-serving desire to be rewarded for believing and doing the right things or to escape punishment for not doing so, then we may recognize the presence and work of the God whom Christians believe was uniquely revealed in Jesus Christ. On the other hand, wherever and among whomever we do not see that kind of religion and morality (including among Christians), then we must say that God in Christ is not yet known at all or has been forgotten or rejected.

Finally, *wherever and among whomever people are being set free* from things that enslave and dehumanize them, we may gratefully recognize the presence and work of the Spirit of the Triune God. "Where the Spirit of God is present, there is freedom, freedom from sin, freedom <u>from</u> the fears and animosities that set family members and people of different races, genders, classes and religions against each other, freedom <u>from</u> self-destructive addictions, to drugs or to narcissistic preoccupations with one's own health or happiness or possessions or even with one's eternal salvation; freedom <u>from</u> the paralyzing despair or freedom <u>from</u> the apathetic resignation that comes from the idea that nothing can ever be different in one's life or this world. Freedom <u>from</u> all that and freedom <u>for</u> new beginnings in personal lives or social situations. On the other hand, wherever and among whomever (including among Christians) there is fearful, hopeless, defensive or worst of all pious acceptance of the way things are, where there is resistance to every attempt to create a more just and compassionate human community because of cynical suspicion that takes for granted that human relationships are doomed by fate, where the pious argument that God has ordained some to be healthy and some sick, and some rich and some poor, and some superior and some inferior, then the Spirit of the Living God whom Christians confess is resisted and not believed in at all."[70]

God is at work in this world, this *whole* world. We forget that sometimes. We need some guidance in finding it. These college kids needed help finding it too. In fact, I had to be careful how I asked these college students about it. They would laugh at me if I didn't explain what I was looking for. "Is there much religious life here on campus?" "Here?! At University Towers Dorm?! Are you kidding? There isn't a lot of religion going on here!" "No, that isn't what I mean." I needed to explain what I was looking for. It takes some thought. It takes time.

When it comes to non-Christians, Christians are most often informed by the Great Commission: "Go therefore," Jesus tells his disciples in Matthew, just days before the ascension, "go therefore and make disciples of all nations, baptizing them and teaching them all i have commanded you." That is The Great Commission. We are called to be evangelists! We forget, though, that we are also compelled, at the very same time, by the Great Commandments. You remember: "You shall love the Lord your God with all your heart, with all your soul and with all your mind, and you shall love your neighbor as yourself." In fact, this is what Jesus refers to in today's scripture. "They who have my commandments and keep them are those who love me. And those who love me will be loved by my father and I will love them and reveal myself to them." The obvious follow-up question is "Well, what *are* his commandments?" And the answer is thus... "You shall love the Lord your God with all your heart, with all your soul and with all your mind, and you shall love your neighbor as yourself." So, we have to abide by both the Great Commission and the Great Commandment. "Those

---

[70] ibid.

who abide in love, abide in God and God abides in love" (I John). That is how we do it. However awkward it might be. That is what we do. We meet friendship with friendship, hostility with kindness, generosity with gratitude, persecution with forbearance, truth with agreement, and error with truth. We express faith with humility and devotion as the occasion requires, whether silently or openly, boldly or meekly, by word or by deed. We avoid compromising the truth on the one hand and being narrow-minded on the other. In short, we welcome and accept others in a way that honors and reflects the Lord's welcome and acceptance of us.[71]

Thanks be to God.

---

[71] The Study Catechism, Presbyterian Church (USA), 1998.

CPSIA information can be obtained
at www.ICGtesting.com
Printed in the USA
LVHW020106280120
645025LV00013B/1253